The spatial contract

MANCHESTER
1824

Manchester University Press

The *Manchester Capitalism* book series

Manchester Capitalism is a series of books which follows the trail of money and power across the systems of our failing capitalism. The books make powerful interventions about who gets what and why in a research based and solidly argued way that is accessible for the concerned citizen. They go beyond critique of neo liberalism and its satellite knowledges to re-frame our problems and offer solutions about what is to be done.

Manchester was the city of Engels and Free Trade where the twin philosophies of collectivism and free market liberalism were elaborated. It is now the home of this venture in radical thinking that challenges self-serving elites. We see the provincial radicalism rooted here as the ideal place from which to cast a cold light on the big issues of economic renewal, financial reform and political mobilisation.

GENERAL EDITORS:
JULIE FROUD AND MICK MORAN

Already published:

The end of the experiment: From competition to the foundational economy

What a waste: Outsourcing and how it goes wrong

Licensed larceny: Infrastructure, financial extraction and the global South

The econocracy: The perils of leaving economics to the experts

Reckless opportunists: Elites at the end of the establishment

Foundational economy: The infrastructure of everyday life

Safe as houses: Private greed, political negligence and housing policy after Grenfell

The spatial contract

A new politics of provision for an urbanized planet

Alex Schafran, Matthew Noah Smith and Stephen Hall

Manchester University Press

The rights of Alex Schafran, Matthew Noah Smith and Stephen Hall to be identified as the authors of this work have been asserted by them in accordance with the Copyright, Designs and Patents Act 1988.

Published by Manchester University Press
Altrincham Street, Manchester M1 7JA

www.manchesteruniversitypress.co.uk

British Library Cataloguing-in-Publication Data
A catalogue record for this book is available from the British Library

ISBN 978 1 5261 4336 5 hardback
ISBN 978 1 5261 4337 2 paperback

First published 2020

The publisher has no responsibility for the persistence or accuracy of URLs for any external or third-party internet websites referred to in this book, and does not guarantee that any content on such websites is, or will remain, accurate or appropriate.

Typeset by
Servis Filmsetting Ltd, Stockport, Cheshire

Contents

List of tables   vi
Preface and acknowledgements   vii

Introduction   1
1   Freedom, reliance and the spatial contract   23
2   Seeing like a system   54
3   Seeing like a settlement   91
4   Reliance and exploitation   114
Conclusion: building a healthy spatial contract   135

Index   153

Tables

1	Six principles of a healthy spatial contract	46
2.1	Traditional understandings of excludability and rivalry	71
2.2	Excludability and rivalry with (Nobel-winning) ideologies	72
2.3	A basic analytical framework for seeing like a system	80
3	Ideologies of reliance systems	110
4	Five faces of oppression in terms of reliance systems	130

Preface and acknowledgements

This book is an attempt to channel the energy and ideas of an incredibly diverse set of thinkers into a usable political, intellectual and analytical framework. It was born of a desire to help critical approaches to the world around us – from political economy, urban studies, geography, philosophy, ecological economics and more – to operationalize that criticality without succumbing to the temptation of ideology. It strives to be generally useful but resolutely non-universalistic.

While it is written by three academics – an urban planner/geographer, a political philosopher and an energy geographer – we worked hard to tone down the argumentation in the text. We tried to make it less academic by generally avoiding debates with existing authors. Some may find this frustrating – points of contention are either ignored, or consigned to the footnotes. We could have written an entire chapter defending our preference for 'vertical approaches', as opposed to horizontal approaches which focus on capitalism or neoliberalism, a decision that will no doubt anger many traditional political economists. We could have cited so many more people, written twice as many words, and engaged more deeply in debate and discussion, but we did not.

There were many reasons behind this decision. Manchester University Press contracted us to write a shorter (and cheaper) book, part of a trend in intellectual publishing that we support. Our goal was to try to articulate a set of ideas, not to

debate with others or prove a point. We were also very con-
scious of who were are – three white men from the USA and
the UK – writing a book of big ideas with a pretentious title
that claims to be generally useful without being universalistic.
We thus focus as much as possible on building upon the great
work of others, rather than debating endlessly. We chose to
cite living scholars doing amazing work whenever possible,
instead of trying to prove our erudition by rehashing the ideas
of long-dead men. When we did focus on those no longer
with us, we focused on brilliant minds such as Elinor Ostrom
and Iris Marion Young who deserve to be in the pantheon,
rather than those who are already there. All three of us find
great value in the traditions of critical political economy, and
consider ourselves allies of so many great critical voices, but
in order to try and produce something we felt was useful we
had to tone down the debate.

This decision to write a pithy, forward-looking book also
means that we skip over many, many things. We list ten holes
in the framework in the conclusion, but obviously there are
many more. A fifth chapter on a spatial analytical framework
would have made sense, considering that two of us are geographers, but this would have taken a book on its own. Each
of us would have added far more detail on our own, but what
you are reading is fundamentally a compromise, a common
space carved out between very different people from very different disciplines.

The authors would like to thank Tom Dark from
Manchester University Press for his long-standing belief in
the project. We would like to thank Karel Williams, Julie
Froud and the late Mick Moran for agreeing to take this
book on as part of the Manchester Capitalism series, and
will forever remember our lone Skype call with Mick before
he passed away far too soon. We would like to thank Julia
Steinberger, Mark Davis, Zac Taylor, Alice Butler, Ricardo
Cardoso and Karel Williams for immensely helpful com-
ments on the draft manuscript. All errors and omissions
remain our own.

A final thanks is due to our families, for incredible support on what became a multi-year transatlantic odyssey. We could not have come anywhere close to this book without you.

Introduction

Let us begin with one of the basic systems that enable life: the water system. Depending on who you are and where you are, the water system will be different. Billions of people every day access water through a complex network of pipes and filters and pumps, often connected to a centralized system of treatment plants and aquifers. For too many people, the system for providing water is inadequate, expensive, unsafe and unreliable, but it is still a system – even if it involves a family member taking buckets down to the river or a well.

We build, rebuild, repurpose and reimagine these water systems, and we do the same with other systems, such as those providing food, housing, healthcare, education, energy, waste disposal and so on. We do this because we rely on these systems. We rely on them not just to live, but in order to be able to act.

Philosophers call the capacity to act our '*agency*'. The first major argument of this book is that our agency is realized in systems we produce and reproduce. Being able to drink or bathe requires systems that provide water. The ability to cook requires systems that provide food, and often systems that provide fuel, stoves and water. The capacity to walk down the road does not just reside in our bodies. It is realized also in the roads we use when we walk down the road. These very roads also require further systems that produce and maintain them. This reliance on systems applies to most of the actions we take on a daily basis. We call all of the systems in which human agency is realized – from the body to electrical grid – *reliance systems*.[1]

You don't make your own reliance systems

Reliance systems are almost always collectively produced, meaning they are rarely provided solely by one person. For example, some of us build our own homes. Some of us grow our own food. Others have solar panels that generate more power than they consume. But even if you live on a farm, or in a self-built home, and so are more involved in producing reliance systems than those who do not live in these ways, this does not mean you made everything you used to build those systems.

After all, even if you built your house, did you harvest and mill the timber? Did you cast the toilets and construct the wind turbines? Did you mine the ore? If you live with a septic tank system instead of a sewer, did you dig the hole and design and construct the lining? Did you learn everything you needed to learn to accomplish these things just from figuring it out, or did you learn it from a family member? Or from books? Or from a school or an apprenticeship programme?

Even in communities where homes are 'self-built' and core reliance systems such as sewerage and water are hard to find, people don't entirely self-provision. Informal settlements are generally collectively built, with complex networks and markets for providing building materials. They too engage larger reliance systems for energy and communication, for food provision, for water and sanitation.[2] In short, people do not self-provision the reliance systems that give us our capacities. Reliance systems are instead collectively provisioned.

By collective we don't mean communal, or state-run, or any particular institutional form. You may be provisioned by your neighbour, your tribe, your local or national government, or by a local, regional or multinational corporation. As we will explain in Chapter 2, we explicitly argue against associating 'collective' with any scale (i.e. local or regional or national) or any type of institutions (state, for-profit, non-profit). By collective we simply mean non-individualistic, bigger than individuals or even households. No matter how independent-minded a person may be, no matter how hard someone works, how much money they make or have, how able or capable they may be, their capacities are produced and reproduced collectively.[3] This isn't meant as a polemical statement, even if many will take it as one. It is simply meant as an important observation of how things actually operate.

Prioritizing reliance systems

If we accept that our agency is realized in reliance systems, and that most reliance systems are collectively produced for most people, we can start to examine the ways in which these systems bind us together. We may or may not enjoy talking to our neighbour, but collective provisioning of reliance systems is *why we have to*. This is true whether things are working or not, whether reliance systems are available to everyone or if some people are cut off, whether some are being exploited, or whether we are providing reliance systems in ways that stay within safe ecosystem limits.

Furthermore, the production and reproduction of reliance systems is not something that only happens in a distant factory or through a minority with specialized skills. To differing degrees depending on a wide range of factors, we are all involved, whether we realize it or not, in the processes by which reliance systems are produced and reproduced. Only at the cost of losing almost all our agency can we escape our *individual* and *collective* roles in the production of reliance systems.

Most reliance systems fit into a simpler term that has become more and more important in recent years: infrastructure. To some, this may mean that they do not belong at the centre of an interesting or important politics. We need the trains to run on time and the water to be clean, but 'real politics' is supposedly about rights and power, sovereignty and global justice, markets and solidarity. Questions about infrastructure are important, but they are often seen as downstream from these issues, or as an input into supposedly more important things.[4]

Yet as a growing chorus of activists, scholars and even politicians are beginning to understand, infrastructure is both long overdue for deeper political attention, and inherently political.[5] In a 2016 essay, the geographer Deb Cowen asks a vital question:

> Could repairing infrastructure be a means of repairing political life more broadly? ... Infrastructure is necessary but the violence it enacts is not. Infrastructure enables all manner of things, and it can foster transformation as well as reproduction.[6]

Cowen is not the only scholar to chronicle how large-scale physical infrastructure, intricate social and legal infrastructure, complex logistics and supply chains, and myriad other components of material life – components of the larger set of structures we call reliance systems – have been at the centre of horrifyingly exploitative and unsustainable practices. Scholars such as Malini Ranganathan, Sapna Doshi, Rosalind Fredericks and many others have shown how infrastructure has been used to produce exploitation and corruption, power grabs and oppression, colonial settlement and racialized domination.[7] Whether it is water systems in Flint or oil pipelines in the Dakotas, the electrical grid in India or food systems in Latin America, virtually every system that enables action and sustains life can *and has been* used to exploit, dominate or oppress.

Reliance systems are also often the source of outsized promises, of imaginations of modernity, progress and development. In their book *The Promise of Infrastructure*, the anthropologists Nikhil Anand, Akhil Gupta and Hannah Appel argue that

> On the one hand, governments and corporations point to infrastructural investment as a source of jobs, market access, capital accumulation, and public provision and safety. On the other hand, communities worldwide face ongoing problems of service delivery, ruination, and abandonment, and they use infrastructure as a site both to make and contest political claims. As the black cities of Michigan or the rubble in Palestine forcefully show, the material and political lives of infrastructure frequently undermine narratives of technological progress, liberal equality, and economic growth, revealing fragile and often violent relations between people, things, and the institutions that govern or provision them.[8]

Yet as Cowen herself points out, these systems can be transformative. In the same essay, she quotes the Ojibwe environmental and political activist Winona LaDuke in explaining her objection to the Dakota Access Pipeline Project, a massive set of pipelines designed to transport shale oil extracted in the Dakotas across the midwestern United States. LaDuke is clear that she is not opposed to pipelines, but simply to *these* pipelines. If the pipelines were being used to carry clean water to people in Flint, whose struggle with lead-tainted water is global news, or to shore up inadequate water and sewerage systems on many Native American reservations, it would be a different story.

The second major argument of this book is that the collective production of reliance systems must be seen as a primary purpose of politics. We use the term 'reliance systems' instead of infrastructure because it makes a more explicit connection between material systems and human agency, but otherwise we find common cause with many such as Cowen who see our political future as rooted in debates about these systems.[9] After all, human agency – the capacity to live one's life – is a matter of core political importance. It isn't enough just to recognize the link between reliance systems and agency, or to recognize the double-edged nature of these systems. If we are to produce a healthier politics, Cowen's first question, about whether reliance systems should be the centre of politics, must be answered, 'Yes.'

From reliance systems to the spatial contract

We call the politics of this relationship between collectively provisioned systems and human agency the *spatial contract*.[10] A spatial contract is an informal or formal agreement governing the production and reproduction of reliance systems. Because these systems enable us to act, the spatial contract is a circular process – the capacities produced by these systems in turn are used to produce and reproduce these system.

There is no single spatial contract, only spatial contracts. Spatial contracts are geographically distinct: there is a spatial contract for transit in Detroit, there is a spatial contract for heat in Malmö, one for housing in Delhi and for telecommunications in Lagos. They are also historically distinct, and have existed for as long as human beings have laboured collectively in some form to produce basic systems. As we work to make clear in Chapter 2, spatial contracts also differ from system to system. Water is not heating, which is not housing, which is not telecommunications.

Our goal in naming spatial contract(s) is to draw attention to them, so that we can better understand them and ultimately build a principled politics around them. The quality of any given spatial contract depends on the terms of the deal. As we explain in more detail in Chapter 1, whether a spatial contract is healthy depends on certain principles. Is a spatial contract producing working and accessible reliance systems? Does it produce the types of capacities it is meant to produce? Is it making the reliance systems stronger? Is the spatial contract exploitative? Are the terms of the deal transparent to all parties? Is it operating within safe ecosystem limits?

This book is an attempt to see politics through the lens of spatial contracts, and to imagine ways to build healthier spatial contracts than those that currently exist in most places. As with any politics, the politics of the spatial contract must include space for resistance and contestation, protest and critical inquiry. The spatial contract must not only create capacities for expressing indignation and challenging the powerful; it must also create capacities for realizing one's more subjective goals, for leisure and fun, for art and aesthetic creation.[11] By focusing on the systems that enable human action, we orient the spatial contract around a *positive* politics of human capacities.

If the politics of the spatial contract is a politics of the provisioning of human agency, then this politics requires the adoption of a broad understanding of what it means for members of communities to be political. As many political theorists have argued, politics goes beyond the formal activity of voting or legislating or protesting, and includes everything from informal debates and discussions to practices of consumption and the mundane activities of everyday life.[12]

Why a spatial *contract*?

The term 'spatial contract' is a reference to one of the best-known concepts in Western political thought: the social contract. The philosophical notion of the social contract, which goes back at least to Thomas Hobbes, is a justification of political authority. The social contract understood in this tradition provides the moral and rational basis for a person to submit to governance by other persons.[13] The animating idea of the philosophical notion of the social contract is that each individual is naturally free, and so ought to have a say about whether they are subject to any form of political domination. Consent to domination is supposed to make that domination morally unproblematic – at least so long as it does not exceed the terms of the agreement. When we extend this idea

to a group of people consenting to being governed by some
institution, we then have a social contract. In theory, a social
contract is a necessary, and according to some, a sufficient
condition for any legitimate political order.

Another contemporary use of the term 'social contract' is
rooted in mid-twentieth-century American labour relations.
This approach focused on the ongoing conflict between
capital – usually the owners of major corporations – and
labour, primarily unions representing workers. The social
contract, conceived this way, did not mean that capital
and labour set aside their differences during this period,
but instead that they developed an informal agreement that
would produce labour peace. During this era wages rose,
economic growth was consistent,[14] and the United States
developed a modern welfare state and saw major investment
by the federal government in highways, mortgages and the
infrastructure of suburbanization. This in turn helped to
vault vast numbers of working-class white Americans into
the middle class. This economic form of social contract was
replicated across post-war Europe in different ways and to
different degrees.

While very different, both of these notions of the social
contract are fundamentally about negotiation and settlement, about effective agreements, both informal and formal.
Neither tradition of the social contract, however, has been
without major flaws and conflicts. Both struggle with issues
of historical and geographical specificity, but in opposite
ways. Both struggle with long legacies of colonialism, racism
and sexism.

The philosophical notion of the social contract seems to
require explicit, informed consent to the authority of not
only the current government but also the whole existing
constitutional order. But does anyone give something like
informed consent to the political order in which they find
themselves? And what is it to consent to the current government when one votes or protests against that government
and its policies?[15] Social contract theory on its own can be

abstract, dehistoricized and ageographical (i.e. utopian in the sense of 'nowhere'). This abstraction, dehistoricization and elimination of geographical specificity in turn allows the philosophical notion of the social contract to serve as a rationalization, or worse justification, of the actions of imperialistic, colonizing, property-owning European men.[16]

The American economic form of social contract was similarly flawed. Despite its widespread adoption in Europe, it is a very historically and geographically specific model.[17] Even more critically, the social contract between labour and capital in the US was tainted by its deeply racist and sexist foundations. African Americans, Latinx Americans and other racialized groups were largely excluded from the social contract, both politically and in terms of benefits. Both the US and European models depended on centuries of brutally violent colonialism.

On these grounds alone we have reason to move past the social contract tradition. Our notion of the spatial contract focuses specifically on developing a more historically, geographically and materially grounded politics, avoiding both philosophical abstraction and the fixation on the generalized economic programme of the post-war North Atlantic. Rather than ignore or rationalize inequalities of different kinds, as we explain in more detail in Chapter 4, our notion of the spatial contract explicitly confronts questions of exploitation and access.

What we do retain from the social contract tradition is the focus on formal and informal agreements as the basis for politics. This is something we have in common with the many contemporary thinkers from different political perspectives who call for a new social contract, or new systems of deliberative democracy.[18] These calls come in the face of growing inequality, rising insecurity, ecological crises, pessimism about democracy and a host of other contemporary problems. For example, Jane Lubchenco, the former president of the American Association for the Advancement of Science, has called for a specific new social contract between scientists and society as part of meeting twenty-first-century environmental challenges.[19] The National Economic and Social Rights Initiative in the United States issued a 2018 call for a new social contract to target inequality that specifically examines local, small-scale and often community-based institutions.[20] In the business community, calls for a new social contract are made in the pages of the *Financial Times* or the conference rooms of the World Economic Forum in Davos.[21] They are often rooted in the specific economic challenges of the digital age – the 'gig economy', automation – or emerge from the social and political challenges of Big Data, privacy, etc. Other versions specifically attempt to address the growing power of corporations, arguing for a new social contract that has three parties – citizens, the state and corporations – in many ways creating a hybrid between the two above understandings.[22]

Other approaches to new social contracts are closer to ours. For example, a group of economists, whose focus is on what they call the 'Foundational Economy', argue specifically for more attention to be paid to the economies we rely on – health and care, electricity and water, the often overlooked 'mundane' economies that we need to survive but that aren't seen to drive competitive economies.[23] In a series of publications, foundational economists have shown both how big and how important the foundational economy is, and how desperately we need a new approach to the political economy of these vital societal functions.[24] As foundational economists are a diverse bunch, their specific political approach varies, with some focused on more traditional citizen–state relations, and others taking a more multi-sectoral approach.

While drawing inspiration from many others who also embrace the importance of negotiating agreements as the basic architecture of good politics, we differ in one important way. Placing reliance systems at the heart of a new social contract demands a contract that is not only social or economic in nature. It must also be material, rooted in the actual systems that we rely upon to act. This material nature of any

new social contract is one of the reasons we term these politics the spatial contact.

Why a *spatial* contract?

We use the term 'spatial contract', as opposed to 'new social
contract', to specifically combine the social and material
nature of these politics.[25] This accomplishes three important
and interrelated things. First, the 'spatial' in spatial contract
signals our intent to develop a political framework that starts
with the particular systems as they are found in the actual
world, in a particular time and place, rather than with a
preconceived political solution. As we have stated previously,
reliance systems are not all the same. River basins, power
grids, sewerage systems and transport networks must be
grappled with on their own terms. Moreover, the same reliance system can be very different in different places. Housing
in Delhi is not housing in Glasgow. Construction materials,
supply chains, cultures of habitation, production techniques
and more are diverse. Thinking in terms of a spatial contract,
rather than simply a social contract, forces us to see both
these material and geographical differences.

Second, recognizing the inherent spatiality of reliance
systems helps us to see these systems in the actual world. As
we develop more fully in Chapter 3, most reliance systems
manifest themselves in the cities and towns and villages of
varying sizes in which the overwhelming majority of people
live. Not only are reliance systems found in these human
settlements, in many ways our settlements *are* intricate
assemblages of reliance systems. Reliance systems and human
settlements are inseparable, and this point is critical for any
potential new politics of reliance systems.

Finally, these two facts – the material and geographical
specificity of each system, and the inherent relationship
between systems and settlements – make it clear that a one-
size-fits-all politics will not suffice. There is no generalized

political solution to the challenges of producing reliance systems. In one country, the nationalization of the energy system may be a good idea, whereas the nationalization of the transport system might be disastrous. Similarly, the privatization of the energy system in one city may be a good idea, but the privatization of the energy system in another city may be a disaster. A system of deliberative democracy in a low-density city with poor transit will be different than one in a high-density city with good transit. The material systems must be animating features of any new politics, not simply a postscript. Building a healthier spatial contract starts with a detailed understanding of the specific system in the specific place at a specific moment in history.

As we hope is clear at this point, our understanding of the spatial contract aims to resist certain totalizing political and economic ideologies. This includes both normative views of how to solve the world's problems and critical viewpoints that claim to identify the primary source of these problems. Both normative and critical ideologies have a tendency to fixate on certain objects, rather than approaching the system in question from the ground up.

This fixation takes three common forms, which we discuss in far more detail in Chapter 2. The first is the tendency to draw political lines around idealized institutions: the state or the market, the commons or private property, the individual or the collective. At other times it is a particular scale: the local or the global, the regional or the national. Sometimes it is to assume that a certain mode of production is the only way to advance human agency. What this reflects is a popular tendency to assume that certain institutions or certain scales or modes of production are inherently better at governing *all* systems in *all* places.[26] Totalizing ideologies can be extremely powerful – and far too tempting – but improving the actual politics of production and reproduction of reliance systems requires a more flexible approach.

One way of thinking about the limits of generalized political solutions is what economists Ben Fine, Kate Bayliss and

Mary Robertson call 'horizontal' approaches to systems. Horizontal approaches can be anything from a set of political economic frameworks (capitalism, socialism, neoliberalism, etc.) to cross-cutting social theories. These approaches are horizontal because they tend to apply their ideologies *across* all or most systems.

Fine, Bayliss and Robertson instead advocate for more 'vertical' approaches. A vertical approach examines systems

> by looking at the full chain of activities underpinning the material production and cultural significance of different goods. As such, the approach avoids over-generalising the relevance of particular factors, instead recognising that any instance of consumption is shaped by a shifting array of context specific determinants.[27]

This approach, known as 'systems of provision', is central to our understanding of spatial contracts. It forces us to recognize that any given spatial contract is unique, and forces us to determine which institution or scale is best for a reliance system by analysing the system itself.

Three interlocking frameworks

In the pages that follow, we work to further develop and explain the core ideas in our understanding of the spatial contract. Chapter 1 delves deeper into the relationship between reliance systems and agency, explaining in more detail how and why reliance systems enable us to act – and how this realizes a meaningful form of human freedom. This chapter also sets down some other important groundwork for the spatial contract. We explain why we believe in a political approach rooted in the idea of a contract, as opposed to other potential approaches focused on collective ownership, a right to the city, or deliberative democracy. We then explain what we mean by a healthy spatial contract, rooting it in six principles.

Chapter 2 is about learning to 'see like a system', stripping away ideological approaches to systems which may fixate on a particular institutional form, sector, scale or so on. We build a framework that highlights how each system is unique, part of our emphasis on system-centred politics, not politics-centred systems. We build this analytical framework using ideas from systems of provisions thinking, socio-technical system research, heterodox and neoclassical economics. We develop a partial set of questions and criteria for analysing different systems.

If Chapter 2 is a framework for pulling apart reliance systems and 'seeing like a system', Chapter 3 is about how and where they come together – in human settlements. 'Seeing like a settlement' is the first step in overcoming the very real political and cultural divisions around which people often assume that systems are divided: between the urban and rural, city and suburb, formal and informal. These political barriers are just as harmful to hopes for a healthier spatial contract as the ideologies discussed in Chapter 2.

Chapter 4 focuses on exploitation and inequality in the provision of reliance systems. We cannot propose a new politics of any kind – let alone a new politics centred in reliance systems – that is not based in acknowledging and overcoming the ways in which much of the world has either been denied access to adequate reliance systems or has had their reliance upon these systems exploited in different ways. Modifying Iris Marion Young's five faces of oppression, we discuss how a healthy spatial contract must reckon with the forms of exploitation and oppression that are so prevalent across the globe.

In the conclusion, we briefly illustrate how using the spatial contract lens informs two import discussions in the contemporary world: the Green New Deal, a vision for combating climate change and economic inequality through a massive retrofit of energy and related systems, and Universal Basic Income, a set of proposals to provide a minimum salary to all persons. We also acknowledge the important and numerous limitations of the book, limitations which point the way towards future interventions in the development of the spatial contract as a framework.

Seen together, this book offers three interlocking frameworks for a new politics of reliance systems. It is an intellectual framework which forces us to see that human agency depends upon material systems that human beings collectively produce and reproduce. It is an analytical framework which provides tools to understand the material and geographical specificity of the production of reliance systems. Finally, it is a political framework which proposes principles that should guide the production of reliance systems.

At the heart of this political argument is a belief that spatial contracts – the relationships between our capacity to act and the systems that realize those capacities – must increasingly become the centre of our politics. Collective provisioning of reliance systems is a fact, not a normative assumption or an ideological stance. As we stated at the outset, one may or may not want to talk to a neighbour or fellow citizen or fellow user of a system, but this is why we have to.

Notes

1 See M. N. Smith, 'Reliance structures: how urban public policy shapes human agency', in D. Boonin (ed.), *The Palgrave Handbook of Philosophy and Public Policy* (Basingstoke: Palgrave Macmillan, 2018), pp. 809–25. We use the term 'reliance systems' as opposed to infrastructure or other possible terms to emphasize the way in which the concept of reliance systems connects socio-technical systems to human action and agency. We explain reliance systems in more detail throughout this chapter and in Chapter 1, and further connect our work to the growing 'infrastructural turn' in the social sciences and public policy throughout the text.

2 See, for instance, recent work by Teresa Caldeira, AbdouMaliq Simone and Edgar Pieterse for a clearer understanding of the complex and intertwined collective economies that produce

self-built housing in cities in the Global South. T. P. Caldeira, 'Peripheral urbanization: autoconstruction, transversal logics, and politics in cities of the global south', *Environment and Planning D: Society and Space* 35.1 (2017), pp. 3–20; A. Simone and E. Pieterse, *New Urban Worlds: Inhabiting Dissonant Times* (Chichester: John Wiley & Sons, 2018).

3 Our notion of collectively produced reliance systems draws from many sources, but one of the most important is the vast literature on 'collective consumption', particularly the work of Jean Lojkine, Manuel Castells and Ray Paul. As explained by Ball, Lojkine's was one of two definitions of 'collective consumption', one that focused on the way in which a good was consumed, either individually or collectively (M. Ball, 'The built environment and the urban question', *Environment and Planning D: Society and Space* 4.4 [1986], pp. 447–64). Like our notion of reliance systems, Lojkine's definition of collective was expansive. In addition to parks, schools, hospitals, roads, public spaces – collective consumption owes its theoretical origins to public goods theory in economics – Lojkine saw housing as collective regardless of ownership or use, due to its embeddedness in the city, an object that could only be consumed collectively. But unlike the early collective consumptionists, our approach argues that it is not the act of consumption that is necessarily collective, but the act of production. Collective consumption in this vein should be the act of consuming necessary goods that must be collectively produced. As While, Jonas and Gibbs point out, collective provision would be more accurate – it is irrelevant whether we consume housing individually or collectively, what matters is the fact that in an increasingly urbanized world, housing must be collectively provisioned (A. While, A. E. Jonas and D. Gibbs, 'The environment and the entrepreneurial city: searching for the urban "sustainability fix" in Manchester and Leeds', *International Journal of Urban and Regional Research* 28.3 [2004], pp. 549–69). See M. Castells and A. Sheridan, 'The urban question: a Marxish approach', *Social Structure and Social Change* 1 (1977); M. Castells, *The City and the Grassroots: A Cross-cultural Theory of Urban Social Movements* (Berkeley, CA: University of California Press, 1983); J. Lojkine, 'Marxist theory of capitalist urbanization', *Estudios Sociales Centroamericanos* 5.15 (1976), pp. 53–78;

B. Théret, 'Collective means of consumption, capital accumulation and the urban question: conceptual problems raised by Lojkine's work', *International Journal of Urban and Regional Research* 6.3 (1982), pp. 345–71.

4 As the political scientist Warren Magnusson points out, one of the grand challenges for reimagining politics is what he calls the 'ontology of the political', i.e. what people think constitutes politics. Since the days of the Greeks, politics has been increasingly seen through the lens of sovereignty and statecraft, of power and rule. For many people, politics means political parties, the state and nation, and anything else is either seen as a small piece of this larger whole, or simply marginalized by the obsessive focus on grander, 'high' politics. W. Magnussen, 'The symbiosis of the urban and the political', *International Journal of Urban and Regional Research* 38.5 (2014), pp. 1561–75 (p. 1562).

5 Thirty-plus years of scholarship have made this clear. For an excellent review, see S. Wakefield, 'Infrastructures of liberal life: from modernity and progress to resilience and ruins', *Geography Compass* 12.7 (2018).

6 D. Cowen, 'Infrastructures of empire and resistance', 25 January 2017, https://www.versobooks.com/blogs/3067-infrastructures-of-empire-and-resistance (accessed 17 October 2019).

7 D. Cowen, *The Deadly Life of Logistics: Mapping Violence in Global Trade* (Minneapolis, MN: University of Minnesota Press, 2014); S. Doshi and M. Ranganathan, 'Contesting the unethical city: land dispossession and corruption narratives in urban India', *Annals of the American Association of Geographers* 107.1 (2017), pp. 183–99; R. Fredericks, *Garbage Citizenship: Vital Infrastructures of Labor in Dakar, Senegal* (Durham, NC: Duke University Press, 2018).

8 N. Anand, A. Gupta and H. Appel (eds), *The Promise of Infrastructure* (Durham, NC: Duke University Press, 2018), p. 3.

9 See also A. Amin and N. Thrift, *Seeing like a City* (Chichester: John Wiley & Sons, 2017).

10 We are not the first to use the term spatial contract, and while we differ significantly in terms of what we mean, there are some key connections to other uses. In a series of publications, the geographer, film-maker and activist Antonis Vradis uses the

term to refer to an informal political agreement, in the tradition of the social contract. But his spatial contract is a very specific understanding in post-dictatorship Athens to allow 'a certain level of rioting and other forms of street-based political contention' in the neighbourhood of Exarcheia, provided that it did not spill into other parts of the city. The spatial contract for Vradis is a tacit understanding emanating from the state that allows a certain period and amount of dissent in certain places and not others, in part to alleviate contradictions or specific tensions. See A. Vradis, 'Athens' spatial contract and the neoliberal omni-present', in M. Mayer, C. Thörn and H. Thörn (eds), *Urban Uprisings* (Basingstoke: Palgrave Macmillan, 2016), pp. 233–51; A. Vradis, 'Terminating the spatial contract', *Society + Space*, 25 June 2012, http://societyandspace.org/2012/06/25/terminating-the-spatial-contract-antonis-vradis/ (accessed 17 October 2019). New Zealander geographers Nicolas Lewis and Warren Moran envision the spatial contract as a more spatialized version of the classic social contract, that is, in terms of relations between the state and its citizens, but with connotations of the post-war social contract. They use the term to describe a breakdown in the post-war, post-colonial social contract in New Zealand that had explicitly spatial principles, including a commitment to spatial equity. This contract broke down – or was broken down – during the neoliberal era, with significant spatial effects in communities across New Zealand. See N. Lewis and W. Moran, 'Restructuring, democracy, and geography in New Zealand', *Environment and Planning C: Government and Policy* 16.2 (1998), pp. 127–53; see also R. A. Kearns, N. Lewis, T. McCreanor and K. Witten, 'The status quo is not an option: community impacts of school closure in South Taranaki, New Zealand', *Journal of Rural Studies* 25.1 (2009), pp. 131–40 for this interpretation of Lewis and Moran. Housing scholars Rowland Atkinson and Sarah Blandy use the term in a way that also describes spatial inequalities, but with a different set of institutional actors at the centre. For Atkinson and Blandy, the spatial contract is an informal politics binding neighbourhoods of different social characteristics, mediated by central and local states, which is threatened by gating and the rise of new forms of income-based segregation. See R. Atkinson and S. Blandy, 'Introduction: international perspectives on the new enclavism and the rise of gated communities', *Housing Studies* 20.2 (2005), pp. 177–86. Quite clearly, all versions of both the spatial and social contract see the contract as both informal and negotiated. While our spatial contract is certainly about institutional relations, we don't focus on any particular sets of institutions, nor on any geographical scale or period in history. Perhaps the most critical aspect we share with prior uses is with Vradis's depiction of a spatial contract that is not necessarily a good thing. As we discuss above, for us the spatial contract is the specific politics of both the virtuous and vicious circle, about the way in which agency derived from reliance systems is used – for good or evil, for sustaining or exploiting, for inclusion or exclusion. The spatial contract is not inherently good, unlike the latter two uses above. The goal is what we call a healthier spatial contract, that is, one that is more virtuous than vicious in its circular nature.

11 The anthropologist James Ferguson asks 'What if politics is really not about expressing indignation or denouncing the powerful? What if it is, instead, about getting what you want?' (J. Ferguson, 'The uses of neoliberalism', *Antipode* 41 [2010], p. 167, quoted in Simone and Pieterse, *New Urban Worlds*, p. 56). The central project in political theory has, since its inception and without interruption, been the articulation and defence of ideal political orders. We can trace this tradition from Plato's *kallipolis* to John Rawls's two principles of justice and up until the present day. Nonetheless, political activity as it is often realized 'on the ground' takes the form of protest far more often than proposal. It is this feature of politics to which Ferguson objects.

12 H. Arendt, *The Human Condition* (Chicago: University of Chicago Press, 1958); J. Habermas, *The Structural Transformation of the Public Sphere*, trans. T. Berger and F. Lawrence (Cambridge, MA: MIT Press, 1989 [1962]); S. M. Okin, *Justice, Gender and the Family*, 3rd edn (New York: Basic Books, 1991).

13 The absence of a social contract is what Hobbes referred to as the 'state of nature', whereby, in his famous words, lives were 'solitary, poor, nasty, brutish and short'. Thomas Hobbes, *Leviathan*, ed. E. Curley (Indianapolis, IN: Hackett, 1994 [1651]), 13.9.

14 In the terms of Thomas Piketty, this was a period notable for having a smaller ratio between the returns to capital and the returns to labour. T. Piketty, *Capital in the Twenty-First Century* (Cambridge, MA: Harvard University Press, 2014).

15 The model of the social contract also assumes independence as our natural condition. The point of the social contract is to preserve and expand this independence through legitimate government. But are human beings really essentially independent creatures, since, after all, we appear to be far more like Aristotle's *zoon politikon* – political animals – than Locke's individuals in the state of nature?

16 For more, see C. Mills, *The Racial Contract* (Ithaca, NY: Cornell University Press, 1997); C. Pateman, *The Sexual Contract* (Stanford, CA: Stanford University Press, 1989); and C. Pateman and C. Mills, *Contract and Domination* (Stanford, CA: Polity Press, 2007).

17 Too often, the North Atlantic post-war experience is used uncritically as a model for development in the Global South. See, for example, J. Robinson, 'Global and world cities: a view from off the map', *International Journal of Urban and Regional Research* 26.3 (2002), pp. 531–54.

18 We also share a good deal in common with political economists and political theorists striving for justice, a right to the city, or what Peggy Kohn calls the 'urban commonwealth' (M. Kohn, *The Death and Life of the Urban Commonwealth* [Oxford: Oxford University Press, 2016]). We are fundamentally motivated by the same injustices, but see more potential in repurposing social contract ideas than other potential pathways. We explain in more detail in Chapter 1 why we favour a contract approach, as opposed to one focused on justice, rights or forms of democracy.

19 J. Lubchenco, 'Entering the century of the environment: a new social contract for science', *Science* 279.5350 (1998), pp. 491–7; K. O'Brien, B. Hayward and F. Berkes, 'Rethinking social contracts: building resilience in a changing climate', *Ecology and Society* 14.2 (2009), http://www.ecologyandsociety.org/vol14/iss2/art12/ (accessed 17 October 2019).

20 'NESRI launches a new social contract promoting bold and transformative community-driven solutions to inequity', https://

www.nesri.org/news/2018/04/nesri-launches-a-new-social-contract (accessed 17 October 2019).

21 J. Hoffer Gittell and T. Kochan, 'A new social contract', Stanford University Press blog, 3 August 2016, http://stanford press.typepad.com/blog/2016/08/a-new-social-contract.html (accessed 17 October 2019); S. Burrow, 'It's time for a new social contract', World Economic Forum, 17 January 2018, https://www.weforum.org/agenda/2018/01/time-new-social-contract-inequality-work-sharan-burrow/ (accessed 17 October 2019); K. Keith, 'We need to build a new social contract for the digital age', *The Guardian*, 4 April 2018, https://www.the guardian.com/commentisfree/2018/apr/04/we-need-to-build-a-new-social-contract-for-the-digital-age (accessed 17 October 2019).

22 A. White, 'Is it time to rewrite the social contract?', Business for Social Responsibility, April 2007, http://www.tellus.org/pub/ Is%20It%20Time%20to%20Rewrite%20the%20Social%20 Contract.pdf (accessed 17 October 2019).

23 The foundational economy is very similar to how we define and imagine reliance systems, and some of our earliest thinking on this issue is included as a working paper on the foundational economy website. See S. Hall and A. Schafran, 'From foundational economics and the grounded city to foundational urban systems', Foundational Economy Working Series paper no. 3, May 2017, https://foundationaleconomycom.files.wordpress. com/2017/01/2foundational-urban-systems-for-mundane-econ omy-3-0213.pdf (accessed 17 October 2019).

24 Foundational Economy Collective, *Foundational Economy. The Infrastructure of Everyday Life* (Manchester: Manchester University Press, 2019).

25 We do not use the term 'spatial' here to imply that the spatial is a substitute for the social in the larger sense, nor to suggest any specific spatial relationship between reliance systems and agency. The spatial is meant to give greater material, geographical and historical specificity to the contracts, but they remain inherently social. Geographers may find it surprising that a book with spatial in the title written by two geographers does not include spatial analysis. Spatial analysis is vital to understanding any given spatial contract, but developing a framework for this remains outside the purview of this book.

26 A. Schafran, 'Debating urban studies in 23 steps', *City* 18.3
    (2014), pp. 321–30.
27 B. Fine, K. Bayliss and M. Robertson, 'The systems of provision
    approach to understanding consumption', in Olga Kravets,
    Pauline Maclaran, Steven Miles and Alladi Venkatesh (eds), *The
    SAGE Handbook of Consumer Culture* (London: Sage, 2018),
    pp. 27–40.

1 Freedom, reliance and the spatial contract

Imagine visiting a crowded marketplace. Are you free to travel through that market? What if there was a law that restricted non-citizens from entering and you were a non-citizen? What if the marketplace had narrow lanes that could not accommodate the wheelchair you use? What if there was an entry fee that you could not afford? What conditions must be met to be free to do something?

In the middle of the twentieth century, the philosopher Isaiah Berlin summarized an account of freedom which he called 'negative liberty' (we use the terms 'liberty' and 'freedom' interchangeably). Drawing on writings such as Thomas Hobbes's famous seventeenth-century definition of liberty as 'the absence of external impediment', Berlin characterized negative freedom as the freedom one has in virtue of the absence of obstruction imposed by others.[1] For example, if you are locked in a jail cell, then the walls, bars, door and locks, among other things, obstruct your ability to exit the cell. You are not free to leave.

Scholars and activists from across the political spectrum followed Berlin in focusing intensely and at times exclusively on negative freedom as the only form of freedom that matters.[2] From libertarians, who treat freedom as the foundational value on which all political questions hinge, to human rights activists, who focus on both state repression of minorities and political opponents and the direct application of violence to bodies, the conception of freedom is typically negative freedom. Freedom to many people is thus freedom as an absence.[3] Freedom is the absence of unfreedom.[4] For example, if unfreedom is the presence of an external impediment, like a boulder blocking a path, then freedom is simply the absence of that boulder.

This approach to thinking about freedom is understandable. So many of the obvious sources of people's suffering have involved the interference of armies, religious institutions, the nobility, state actors, and so on. For example, the freedom to practise religion was for centuries compromised by direct intervention by the Church or by state persecution. It makes sense to treat the presence of 'negative freedoms' as a crucial component of freedom.

Yet there is more to the boulder than wishing it wasn't blocking the path. When a boulder impedes one's path, when laws forbid behaviour, when one is dominated by another and so must ask their permission to live in any number of ways, what is lost is the ability to lead one's life in some desired or valued way. What is lost is the capacity to take actions that one wants or values. When someone is unfree, they cannot do what they want. What is compromised by unfreedom, then, is one's capacity to act. Philosophers use the word 'agency' to refer to this capacity to act. External impediments, legal prohibitions, domination and so on are forms of unfreedom because they are ways to limit human agency. So, if loss of freedom is the limitation of human agency, then freedom is human agency. That is, to be free is to be able to act.

Unfortunately, capacities to act do not spring into existence when impediments or restrictions are removed. Other conditions must be met. For example, a law prohibiting walking down the road limits my capacity to walk down the road. Yet regardless of what the law says, if there is no road to walk on, then I cannot walk down the road anyway. When it comes to reliance systems, people are free not only because of an absence of laws or customs or rules or armed guards obstructing them, but because of the presence of a specific reliance system. In order to have the capacity to walk down the road, there needs to be a road.

In this chapter we first expand upon the philosophical foundations of this more material or active understanding of freedom, an understanding that owes the deepest debt to the capabilities approach developed by Amartya Sen, Martha Nussbaum and others. We then focus on explaining in more depth what we mean by reliance systems, sketching out their general features, their complexity, their generally co-produced nature and their multi-dimensionality.

We then address the question of how to think about the politics of reliance systems. We briefly touch on other approaches, and then develop an approach based on a modification of social contract thinking. We refer to this as *the spatial contract*. As a spatial contract, like a social contract, can be both healthy and unhealthy, we end by setting out six principles for producing *healthier* spatial contracts.

The capabilities approach

Variously rooted in Aristotelian thought about human capacities or Marxist thought about the material conditions of the proletariat, many have developed and defended understandings of freedom not in terms of an absence but instead in terms of the presence of abilities. For example, Karl Marx wrote that '"free activity" is for the communists the creative manifestation of life arising from the free development of all abilities'.[5] He and Engels wrote that to be free 'in the materialistic sense' is to be 'free not through the negative power to avoid this or that, but through the positive power to assert true individuality'.[6] For Marx, the central question of freedom was not 'what must one avoid to be free' but instead 'what abilities must one have to be free?'

Amartya Sen developed a contemporary interpretation of freedom along these lines. Sen began through an interrogation of John Rawls's views about social justice, and, in particular, what Rawls called *social primary goods*: income, wealth and the social bases of self-respect.[7] Sen argued that while these are surely important, they are poor indices of well-being.[8] According to Sen, there is huge difference between the well-being one enjoys by virtue of being wealthy, and the well-being one enjoys by virtue of not being immobilized by a serious illness. Lacking the ability to move from place to place cannot be directly 'made up for' by increasing someone's income and wealth. Furthermore, people differentially convert resources to actions and to capacities.

The resources required for a growing child to be able to play, for example, are different from those required for a full-grown adult to play, and the resources required for an *ill* growing child to be able to play are different from those required for a healthy child. Sen generalizes this point to cover limitations on converting resources to capabilities due to social forces, environmental factors and so on. Women in most societies, for example, remain hampered by sexism even if they gain income and wealth.[9]

These reflections drive Sen to conclude that we cannot de-link freedom from well-being, which is what Rawls and those following him did.[10] We should instead try to understand well-being at least partially in terms of freedom.[11] We should accept as a starting point, for example, that being healthy is better than being ill.

Sen's approach has come to be called the *capabilities approach*.[12] This approach defines a person's freedom as their 'capability set', or the set of actions a person can perform in their life. For example, if you walk to your car, then drive that car to the airport, buy a ticket to fly to another city, and then board that plane and fly to that other city, then one's capability set includes, among many other things, the ability to walk, the ability to drive a car, the ability to drive to the airport, the ability to buy something, the ability to board a plane and so on. Whether someone takes advantage of these capabilities is up to that person. What is important is that people can choose whether to realize a capability at all. In that respect, they are free.[13]

A person's capability set is not fixed only by what they are *legally* permitted to do. Sen emphasizes that 'personal characteristics and social arrangements' are crucial, too.[14] Factors such as income and wealth, as well as other resources such as access to technology, are necessary for freedom. But at a certain point, more income or new technologies do not appreciably expand a person's capability set. The marginal increase in capabilities drops to zero. In this way, we have a means of making sense of when adding or removing resources from a person's life makes them freer or not.[15]

This reveals that freedom understood in terms of capabilities is more comprehensive than the negative freedom approach. The threat to capabilities that a disabling injury poses cannot be characterized exclusively in terms of external impediments or state domination or employment restrictions. Even if the state positively affirms the right to live as the disabled person prefers, and even if no one stands in the way of that person's desires, the disabled person's hope to live in a world that accommodates her condition remains unfulfilled.[16]

Sen's approach was extended by Martha Nussbaum, who, like Sen, judged the morally basic consideration to be the lives that we can live: 'the key question to ask, when comparing societies and assessing them for their decency or justice, is, "What is each person able to do and to be?"'[17] This approach, Nussbaum says, 'is *focused on choice or freedom*, holding that the crucial good societies should be promoting for their people is a set of opportunities, or substantial freedoms, which people then may or may not exercise in action: the choice is theirs'.[18]

The capabilities approach also provides a new way of thinking about unfreedoms. Unfreedoms can be seen as socially produced 'incapabilities'. If some social force makes women incapable of participating fully in the economy, that is an unfreedom. And if some social force makes people incapable of expressing certain political views, then that is also an unfreedom.[19] Unfreedoms are eliminated not merely by *removing* whatever social conditions produce the incapability but by *producing* the capability itself. This attention to the production of capacities is central to our account of the spatial contract.

From capabilities to reliance systems

Nussbaum and Sen treat the capacity to act – agency – as an essentially *corporeal* phenomenon. Actions are realized entirely in the human body. This helps to explain why they focus on corporeal limitations to capability: physical disabilities requiring persons to be in wheelchairs, differing protein needs between adults and children, differing needs of the non-pregnant and the pregnant, threats to physical health posed by malaria and other diseases, and so on.

Capabilities in this view are a limited set grounded in conceptions of what a human body can do.[20] Their understanding of capabilities is thus rooted in the bodily ideal of 'being adequately nourished, being in good health, avoiding escapable morbidity and premature mortality, etc., to more complex achievements such as being happy, having self-respect, taking part in the life of the community, and so on'.[21] What justice requires, on this view, are policies supporting the body and conditioning the environment to fit that body, however it is manifested, where the aim is to ensure that these capabilities are realized in the body. Nussbaum and Sen therefore emphasize broad policies such as building up and expanding public health programmes, policing violence in interpersonal relationships and expanding education as the aim of any acceptable capabilities approach to justice.[22]

Yet neither Sen nor Nussbaum ask about human agency itself.[23] What is human agency? Answering this question tells even more about what freedom is than the formal characterization of freedom as a capability.

Let's return then to the road, to the question raised earlier:

what is it to be free to walk down the road? Most people would agree that this requires at least being free legally and socially, and Sen and Nussbaum have helped make us sensitive to the fact that we must also be physically capable of doing so, in the sense that our bodies need to be able to walk down the road. Yet to truly understand what makes someone free to walk down the road, we need to start paying a lot more attention to the road.

The road – or whatever surface it is on which a person moves, whether on foot or in a wheelchair or through whatever mode of transport – must be produced and maintained. To be truly useful, it must be connected to other roads and pathways, to homes and businesses and places people need to go. The seemingly simple capacity of being able to walk down the road requires more than laws (or the absence of laws) and a certain bodily condition. It also requires, at the very least, road-supplying and road-maintaining systems.

Consider also the capacity to cook dinner. This capacity depends not merely on the legal right to cook a hot dinner, and is not realized merely in one's body properly functioning, or even the provision of ingredients. It is also realized in the capacity of the stove to cook. If someone's stove does not work, then that person cannot cook dinner, no matter what the law says or how healthy they are. In this way, the stove's capacity is as much an element of the capacity to cook dinner as any bodily capacity or legal right. Furthermore, the capacity to cook dinner extends beyond the stove. The stove cannot function if proper fuel for that specific type of stove is not available. The capacity to cook is realized not just in the law and in the body, but in all the *reliance systems* that make cooking possible.

Reliance systems do not help us to manifest capacities to act. They *are* those capacities (sometimes we will call these 'agential capacities' to highlight the connection to agency). People do not have the capacity to cook in the absence of functional tools for cooking. People do not have the capacity to cycle down a road in the absence of functional bicycles and navigable roads. Working tools, working bicycles, working

roads and working bodies are not merely instruments for
action. They are the systems that constitute (or realize) the
capacities to perform these actions. Our abilities to live
are realized in material systems, from the simple, such as a
path through a wood, to the complex, such as infrastructure involving millions of parts, connections, nodes, inputs,
workers and governing structures.[24] While individuals have
certain abilities, they are realized in systems that go well
beyond the individual. If we understand human freedom in
terms of human agency, then we can see that human freedom
is realized in systems located across space and place – from
our bodies to far-flung power plants.[25]

The nature of reliance systems

What we have just presented is a view of human freedom
understood as an assemblage of material and social systems.
This extension of the capabilities approach is the foundation
of our argument for a renewed focus on the politics of provisioning these systems. The next step is to think more critically
about the nature of these systems.

First, we should avoid the habit of seeing objects such as
bridges and roads, or stoves and fuel delivery infrastructure,
as simple, permanent, static objects. As we discuss in more
detail in Chapter 2, we must see them as active, evolving,
social and technical systems. All these 'objects' are in constant flux, both internally and relationally. Internally, they
suffer decay. For example, roads degrade, stoves rust, fuel can
evaporate or rot or leak. Relationally, their functional roles
can change. Computers become obsolete when data storage
systems radically change or the computing power required by
applications increases. A parking space can become a small
park, a road can become a parking lot.

None of the freedoms constituted by these reliance systems
are stable and permanent. Not only must these systems be
made in the first place before action is possible, they must

be maintained, rebuilt, sustained and reoriented all the time. We can represent reliance systems graphically and statically, as we do a musical score, but their reality is in their performance, which always unfolds over time, in space, and with a material specificity.[26]

Although labour is constantly expended in the production, reproduction and transformation of reliance structures constituting human agency, this isn't always visible, especially in highly urbanized areas. The effort of maintenance is often obscured – by distance, by time, by efficiency, or simply because we are not paying attention. Too often we only see the labour involved in these systems when they break down or are inadequate – we see the labour of water when it is associated with people moving potable water in tankers and jugs, not the work done far away or underground. We see labour when contestation erupts, when systems are struggled over,[27] even if the operations and transformations of reliance systems constituting human freedom are rarely at rest. They are always being re/produced.

As we strove to make clear in the introduction, one of the most vital aspects of the production and reproduction of the overwhelming majority of reliance systems is that it is collective, not individualistic. Not only are reliance systems produced by people working together, they are also built on historical efforts. When a doctor swabs a patient's arm with alcohol to inject insulin, the doctor is combining distillation technology developed by Arab scientists in the middle ages with a Canadian discovery in the 1920s and more recent biotechnology innovations that use recombinant DNA to synthesize insulin, so that we don't have to extract it from a dog's pancreas, as the original Canadian scientists did.

Two dimensions of reliance systems

As an analytical tool, we can also divide reliance systems along two dimensions.[28] The first dimension is what we have been focusing on so far: the system producing and reproducing human activity. Let us call this the *material component*, recognizing that this is shorthand for systems of re/production that also incorporate certain social aspects. We can talk about the paint and the asphalt as the material of a reliance system partially constituting the capacity to ride a bike on a city street, but this is shorthand for the whole system that re/produces the paint, the asphalt, and the paint being put on the asphalt in ways that mark out a cycle lane.

Reliance systems can also be defined in terms of what agential capacity they produce. We will call this second dimension of reliance systems the *functional component*. For example, if asphalt is a material component of a reliance system, the actions that it enables are walking, driving, cycling and so on. These are the different functions for which the asphalt can be recruited in order to constitute a reliance system.

This separation allows us to appreciate that the material component of a reliance system is not 'naturally' linked to some activity. The same material can be 'for' many activities, that is, it can be *recruited* for many different functions. A very simple example would be the material of a hammer recruited for the function of hammering nails into wood, and the same material being recruited as a paperweight, a weapon, or to dismantle rather than construct. A more complex example is how the material of a house can be used for the function of being a domicile for a family, or (along with other material) for the function of storing wealth. Depending on the ownership structure of the material house, different actors may perform each function, or they may be the same actors. These two functions can be symbiotic, or they can be in conflict with each other. When a landlord sells a house and evicts tenants, the two uses are in conflict.

Another case involves small shifts in the internal features of the material. A strip of asphalt in a busy city centre can be recruited for the activity of driving cars, as we have the capacity to drive a car in the city partially in virtue of the existence of this strip of asphalt. If flexible posts and paint are added to the asphalt, thereby creating a cycle lane, then the material – the asphalt, the posts, the paint – will be recruited for the end of riding a bicycle. This is how a more expanded agential capacity of riding a bicycle is produced and rooted in an urban space. In this case, the asphalt, the posts and the paint are all (partially) the material of this particular capacity to ride a bicycle in the city.[29] Roughly the same material – the road – can be a technology for walking, biking, driving, selling food, racing, protesting, making profit, transporting goods, dividing people, uniting people, imposing rule, building power, separating space and so on, often simultaneously.

A similar story can be told for the material components of mass transit systems. In addition to having the aim of moving people through a city, they can also realize the activities of commerce, politics with other members of the public, performance and so on (just consider all the activities other than transporting themselves that people use mass transit systems for). *Highly flexible* material such as roads can be recruited for many different ends, in that many capacities can be realized in them. *Highly specific* material such as WiFi modems can often be recruited for very few ends, in that only very few agential capacities can be realized in them.

There are subtle material differences between the ways in which heterogeneous capacities are realized in highly flexible material. These differences matter. They are often cynically exploited, as when a politician objects to building cycle lanes by saying that someone can ride a bicycle on city streets even when cycle lanes don't exist. The fact that many capacities share the material in which they are realized is critical, especially to the politics of these systems, which is the focus on this book. This flexibility ends up being the basis for conflict and struggle as much the basis for improvisation, efficiencies and common cause.

For example, the distinction between the material and functional components of a reliance system reveals how substitutions of material can sometimes prevent the loss of freedom. This is dependent on the materiality of the system.

If wheat is not available for bread production, people can substitute rice or another starch, or meat or vegetables, in order to realize that simplest of capacities: the capacity to nourish oneself. But if some material element of the system of insulin production is not available, a diabetic cannot substitute with antibiotics or cancer medicine. A gas oven cannot burn electricity, a nuclear plant cannot use coal, but an electrical power grid can accept electricity from different sources regardless of fuel source. Thus the degree of substitutability of the material constituting a reliance system becomes evident once we separate the material component from the functional component, a fact we discuss in more detail in Chapter 2.

Why some material was produced need not determine its dominant purpose. Rather, it is how the material is recruited that determines its function, and thus what sort of reliance structure it is. A road may be built for cars, but cyclists might take it over, leaving no room for cars. As our focus is on the politics of reliance systems, it is essential not to treat the process of recruiting material for different functions as a 'natural' process, in the way that seeds naturally take root in soil. Rather, it is a political process, and subject to contestation.

Thinking about reliance systems in this way avoids the tendency to imagine that there are certain capacities that people 'naturally' have in virtue of certain materials being available to them. Just because something has been built, it does not follow that it will be recruited for a specific agential function. Consider again the example of housing. While it may seem 'natural' that the building itself ought to be recruited for the sake of agential capacities associated with daily living – sleeping, washing, eating and so on – the building is also often recruited for the activities of storing capital, generating revenue, light industrial production, commerce and much more. In highly flexible reliance systems such as housing, a vast diversity of agential capacities can (and likely have been) constituted in the same material component. Which agential capacities are realized in that material – and thus which freedoms are realized – depends upon what ends that material is recruited for.

The spatial contract

As we explained briefly in the introduction, we use the term 'spatial contract' to refer to the set of negotiated agreements, both formal and informal, that govern the collective re/production and management of reliance systems. Because their focus is on reliance systems, which always have some material component, spatial contracts are essentially tied to the materiality of human agency. They are grounded in *stuff*. They are often, at least to some degree, visible in the built environment.

They are also grounded in the social realities of the specific system, its geography and history. The spatial contract includes the purposes and values of the reliance systems being re/produced, who has standing to intervene in the processes of production, what interventions are possible or considered appropriate or inappropriate. It includes which social positions are constructed along with these processes, and the rights, duties and other legal incidents that define those positions. A spatial contract is not static, and there may be spaces for renegotiation or insurrection.

Like social contracts, a spatial contract is, in its broadest terms, an agreement between persons, between persons and political institutions, and/or between institutions themselves. Unlike traditional accounts of social contract theory, which treat political engagement as a way to mitigate threats of violence or as a way to establish a lasting formal settlement (such as a written constitution or a set of laws), the spatial contract locates the urgency of political engagement in the fact that reliance systems must be produced and reproduced collectively and constantly.

The complex materiality of reliance systems – the way

that they can be transformed through shifts in function and context, their very specific nature, their tendency to move rapidly from a state of order to one of disorder – gives most spatial contracts a constantly evolving character. Unlike traditional social contracts, which are thought to be highly stable, spatial contracts, because they are centred on the production of reliance systems, shift as reliance systems change. As a road decays or as its functions transform, the spatial contract centred on that road shifts with it. There is no way to fix, for any meaningful period of time, a formal universal settlement governing the production of reliance systems, since reliance systems are always in flux. We are constantly called to the table to engage with each other to settle the terms of the re/production and management of reliance systems.[30]

One might approach the need for a new politics of reliance systems through other traditions than the social contract. Why not talk in terms of rights or justice? Can one not appeal to a right to freedom? A just distribution of capabilities? What about certain political systems rooted in deliberative democracy, or forms of engagement, or collective ownership, which have been proven to be useful in producing better housing or food or water?

In the following sections, we first briefly review these other approaches, highlighting both their vital contributions and their limitations *as an overarching framework*. We then explain in more detail why we have chosen to modify social contract theory to form this notion of the spatial contract, and how it differs from the various historical and contemporary traditions of social contract thinking. Finally, we develop six principles for determining whether or not an existing spatial contract is healthy or unhealthy. These principles underlie an analytical framework for understanding spatial contracts in a non-ideological way, the development of which is the core focus of Chapters 2–4.

Ownership, rights, justice, deliberative democracy

One traditional approach to resolving the challenges of pro-ducing and reproducing reliance systems is to advocate for the collective ownership of all things, especially the means of production. This approach attempts to invest in each person an equal share of political control over the systems that re/produce their agency. Collective ownership struggles with questions of why heterogeneous ownership arrangements are deployed in production. If we focus on understanding systems (Chapter 2) and not just their outputs – that is, the entirety of the system for the production of housing, and not just the house – we find a diversity of terms of tenure, forms of ownership and control, building cultures, sources of materials, and property rules governing the interconnections between systems. We can both affirm that radical reforms to existing relationships of property are needed and insist that these reforms take seriously the historically, geographically and materially specific character of each system of produc-tion.[31] This suggests that a simple model of collective owner-ship is either too abstract an ideal or too disengaged from actual demands of production to be a complete model of how reliance systems should be produced.

The call for a right to the city is another common approach popular in both activism and academic circles. A right to the city is, broadly speaking, not a right to live in a city or a par-ticular place, but to effectively participate in the production of that settlement. The right to the city can include everything from the right to vote and participate in formal processes to the right to self-built housing and actual material engagement with systems. This approach is powerful but incomplete. For, while the right to the city approach underlies one of the six principles by which we analyse the health of a spatial contract, its focus on governance at a certain scale obscures how reliance systems can be transnational just as much as they can be rooted in a single neighbourhood. For this reason, among others, we do not think the right to the city *on its own* provides a deep enough framework for developing a politics of how reliance systems must be produced, reproduced and maintained.

A similar and more technical approach can be found in familiar models of deliberative democracy.[32] The central idea behind these models is to move away from simple systems of preference aggregation (democracy conceived of as 'the kind of behaviour that is appropriate in the market place')[33] and towards democracy in which 'public deliberation of free and equal citizens is the core of legitimate political decision-making and self-governance'.[34] This approach seeks ways to transform private preferences into commitments born of engagement within a variety of public spheres.[35] These public spheres are constituted in part by norms requiring, on at least one influential account, that 'justification of the terms and conditions of [political] association proceeds through public argument and reasoning'.[36] As a result, participants develop capacities for, as Seyla Benhabib puts it, 'reasoning from the point of view of others'.[37] This is a model of reason as a capacity for impartial engagement with and assessment of lines of argument around policy questions. In a deliberative democracy, then, the aim is to substitute, as Jon Elster puts it, 'the language of interest with the language of reason'.[38]

Deliberative democracy, while important, faces several difficulties that the spatial contract aims to avoid. First, we resist reducing all questions of *governance* to questions of *government*. There is no ideal system for re/producing and managing reliance systems – some should be re/produced or managed by the state, others via market processes, others via mixed systems. In at least some cases, market mechanisms, private negotiations and so on might be more efficient and inclusive mechanisms for facilitating the production and reproduction of reliance systems. Statecraft, after all, is often exclusionary.

Second, the legal structures, and especially the formal rights, that guarantee citizens participation in democratic governance must be realized materially. A deliberative forum is not democratic if the physical space for deliberation is too small to accommodate all who wish to participate, or if the communication system is so fragile that it collapses under the weight of mass civic engagement.[39] Insofar as theorists of deliberative democracy even consider these issues, they treat them as afterthoughts. But they are not afterthoughts. For the capacities to deliberate collectively – however constrained or constructed so as to meet the requirements of a democratic ideal – are not merely psychological. They are realized in material reliance systems that must be produced and reproduced. Any model of deliberative democracy must take this seriously.

Third, while technical questions may always be political, that does not make them any less technical. Conscientious and earnest participation in democratic governance therefore requires substantial training and dedication to understanding the particularities of each technical question. Most people have neither the time nor the inclination, to say nothing of the ability, to meet these demanding standards for every single technical issue. Informed decision making may require ceding authority to those with the relevant knowledge and skill. It may seem that we can just decide that everyone ought to have heated homes, but further decisions about how the heating systems will be constructed and operated cannot be settled without expertise. And yet how these questions are settled determines the scope of people's freedom at least as much as the more general one about the necessity of heated homes.

Finally, reliance systems are not static. They decay over time. They must be constantly reproduced through direct reconstruction, changes in management practices and so on. The materials of reliance systems are constantly recruited for new aims, and so new reliance systems bloom out of existing ones.[40] This may require shifting governance frames, and often requires seeing new populations as engaging with the reliance system, and so realizing new freedoms. The geographical distribution of a reliance system can become increasingly uneven as population shifts. This can require wholesale review of the governance of these systems. In all these cases and more, the settlement governing the production and reproduction of reliance systems must be seen as constantly evolving. The production and reproduction of these settlements, with their shifting subjects, geographies, populations and technical requirements, among other factors, are not amenable to a single form of governmentality.

A spatial contract therefore does not eschew the ideals of deliberative democracy. But since it is focused on the re/production of reliance systems, it places the materiality of these systems front and centre. From the recognition that the capacities employed in democratic deliberation must be produced materially to the stubborn material and historical specificity of the systems being governed by the spatial contract, centring a politics around reliance systems imposes distinctive limitations on the possibilities for transformation of the 'contracts' governing the re/production and management of those reliance systems.

Principles of a healthy spatial contract

The spatial contract involves the development of iterated, loose, flexible and negotiated agreements between people, institutions and the various permutations of both to produce reliance systems, many of which are required for the re/production and management of other reliance systems. The spatial contract is therefore a nested and constantly evolving series of collective settlements governing the re/production and management of human freedom. In this way, our repurposing of the social contract into the spatial contract places at the centre questions about how reliance systems interact, how they support one another, how they infiltrate or diminish one another, and how they are harnessed for the re/production of each other. These interactions, when functioning well, re/produce and expand human freedom. Sometimes, though, they limit or destroy it. Over time spatial contracts shift as reliance systems and the conditions of their re/production transform. A spatial contract is therefore highly specific to space, time, history and culture. This means that we cannot make universal claims or draft a constitution to be applied everywhere.

What we can do is specify key principles of a healthy spatial contract. We offer six principles as the core of our understanding about what a healthy spatial contract looks like. We do not intend this list to be final, but merely a good place to begin, a way of anchoring the spatial contract morally, and of evaluating whether any given spatial contract is healthy or unhealthy.

Three points are worth bearing in mind. First, a healthy spatial contract is not merely a contract yielding rights and privileges. It also yields duties and liabilities. In particular, people must use the agency enabled by spatial contracts either to participate in making new spatial contracts and/ or to use the existing reliance systems in productive ways. Second, whereas reliance systems are collectively produced, the spatial contract governs the agency of both individuals and institutions. Hence the principles below apply both individually and collectively. Finally, these principles are not absolute principles that require perfection, nor are they threshold principles establishing a minimally justifiable condition. Rather they are range principles. Much as with health, there is no absolute condition of perfection, but rather a vast range between healthier and less healthy.

Principle one: core purpose must be retained
Housing that is empty but profitable is not housing. It is a reliance system realizing the capacity to produce wealth. A transit system built only to open land up for development is not for transit. It is a reliance system realizing the capacity to develop land for other purposes.

Since the material of a reliance system can be recruited for multiple reliance systems – a underground train can be a reliance system for transit, for commerce, for rest, for shelter and so on – there is good reason to expect that producers of reliance systems allow for multiple uses. However, the production of a house must produce capacities for the new users of the home, not only the builder, the financier, the permitting official or the landscaper.

The financialization of real estate has made this clear. The extension of credit on its own has proven essential to provision housing. Yet as finance has increasingly grown into a vast system of its own, the operation of these systems can increase one group's capacities to purchase housing while reducing another group's capacities to access housing. The production of reliance systems that represent themselves as realizing some capacity but that threaten to reduce or destroy that same capacity must be viewed suspiciously. There is no way to resolve a settlement around the re/production of a reliance system when people are deceived about the ways in which that system shapes human agency. Spatial contracts that have this feature are therefore unhealthy.

Principle two: the system must be strengthened
Any spatial contract that undermines the very systems that it governs is unhealthy. Any healthy spatial contract should seek to strengthen reliance systems socially and materially. This is distinct from the previous principle because this principle identifies downstream, and not constitutive, features of a spatial contract. Whereas the financialization of housing is sustained only if people are denied housing (in the same way that for-profit health insurance requires that people are regularly denied medical care), this principle concerns itself only with spatial contracts that, as it were, sow the seeds of their own destruction.

Consider global grain production. Current intensive farming practices leach, compact and waste soils, over-apply fertilizer, cause catastrophic insect/pollinator losses, and disregard soil health to the degree that UN officials claim that the world has less than 60 harvests left.[41] While for the moment intensive farming practices might satisfy principle one, they undermine the material foundations of the system. What is required is the opposite: the production, operation and reproduction of critical reliance systems ought to aim to strengthen themselves and other critical systems. A new spatial contract for grain production, or by extension the system providing grain-based foods, is desperately needed.

Principle three: access and inclusion
A healthy spatial contract ensures that the re/production of reliance systems is always at least in part for the sake of extending freedom to others. Collective production cannot be selfishly aimed by producers entirely at the goal of increasing only their own capacities. A healthy spatial contract must aim at facilitating the broadest possible access to reliance systems.

For example, changes to a water system that result in users being cut off are, all else being equal, a feature of an unhealthy spatial contract, as would be changes that make users' access to regular or affordable water more precarious. This principle can also apply to relationships between systems. For example, access to quality education in most places requires access to housing. Thus a spatial contract that denies access to housing also denies access to education.

Principle four: human exploitation must be eliminated
When an agential capacity is especially foundational and urgent, it is easy for the provision of the reliance systems realizing those capacities to be sites for exploitation. For example, the provision of the capacity to consume water often becomes a site for exploitation, such as price gouging and profiteering. Similarly, the capacities to look after one's health and to manage daily under conditions of frailty, both of which are realized in the healthcare system and the social care system, are prime locations for the emergence of exploitative conditions.

As a general rule, the more basic the agential capacity, the easier it is for the provision of reliance systems realizing that capacity to be fraught with some form of exploitation.

Because newer capacities such as those associated with access to the internet, for example, can become foundational for many other non-foundational capacities such as accessing government services, the provision of the reliance systems realizing these capacities can be sites for intensive exploitation as well.

Principal five: planetary boundaries must be respected

A healthy spatial contract retrofits existing reliance systems so that they respect planetary boundaries.[42] We have already argued that the re/production of agency should not result in the destruction of either itself or of other capacities. But it should also not destroy entire ecosystems. It should not impoverish existing or future generations, who will bear the brunt of the consequences of going well beyond planetary boundaries. This is a practical requirement as much as a moral one.

For example, while it might be entirely possible to satisfy the other principles of a healthy spatial contract locally, a cheap, accessible power system running on coal and oil transgresses the atmosphere's ability to cycle CO_2 fast enough to retain a stable climate. By committing to this principle, we commit to deep, structural changes to many if not all reliance systems. There are multiple intersecting ecological crises such as climate breakdown, a 'sixth extinction' event brought about by habitat destruction, and the aforementioned soil health emergency which demand rapid and far-reaching changes to a huge number of spatial contracts.

Principle six: spatial contracts must be transparent[43]

A healthy spatial contract is one in which systems do not hide how they function from parties that want to understand them. This principle goes beyond the mere publication of the relevant bureaucratic paperwork. If you have an energy system, part of the spatial contract governing that energy system is about the decisions made in that system, where to put the power stations, what fuel is to be used. People who want to be a part of that system should be able to gain the knowledge to participate. In an unhealthy spatial contract, those who possess expertise or can and want to gain expertise in the re/production or management of a reliance system are excluded from the construction of the spatial contract for that system.

Since reliance systems are complex, it is unrealistic to ask all parties to understand all aspects of the system. Any expert in any reasonably 'advanced' energy market will freely admit to not understanding the 'whole' system. In this absence of total expertise in any sector, what is needed instead is at least a clear articulation of the terms of the deal, that is, a general characterization of the terms of the spatial contract governing the re/production of that reliance system. This includes making accessible how a spatial contract performs against the other five principles.

There are clear overlaps between the different principles, and they are not intended to be either definitive or mutually exclusive. The question of planetary boundaries impacts questions of access, both for present and future victims of our failure to adhere to this principle. The degree to which a system is strengthened impacts its ability to increase access, and increasing access without strengthening can be dangerous.

We recognize that these principles can also be in conflict, a subject we discuss but do not resolve, as it is too involved for the basic framework that this text is designed to provide. For example, extending electricity access to the rural poor by connecting them to a fossil-fuelled energy grid only expedites climate breakdown, which might very well destroy the same communities' water system. Providing more and more people with grain from the current industrialized farming model only accelerates biodiversity loss, disrupts the nitrogen cycle and depletes soil health further.

Particularly when arguing for extending access we must acknowledge the balancing acts and trade-offs involved in a global community. There is no healthy spatial contract that

Table 1 Six principles of a healthy spatial contract

Principle	Healthy	Unhealthy
1 The retention of core purpose	To what extent is the reliance system achieving what it is explicitly for?	To what extent is the reliance system serving ends that are obscured or hidden?
2 Strengthening the system	To what extent is the reliance system being strengthened? To what extent are system users actively engaged in its positive re/production?	To what extent is the reliance system being weakened? To what extent are system users actively engaged in its negative re/production?
3 Access and inclusion	To what extent does the system extend access and confer/protect the freedoms and agential capacity of others?	To what extent does system restrict access, remove freedoms or retain priority access?
4 The elimination of exploitation and oppression	To what extent is the agency realized in reliance systems produced in a manner that is not exploitative of users, or does not rest on exploitation of others involved in the production of the system?	To what extent is the agency realized in reliance systems produced in a manner that is exploitative of users, or rests on exploitation of others need for the reliance system?
5 The honouring of planetary boundary	To what extent is the agency realized in reliance systems retrofitting existing reliance systems so that they respect planetary boundaries?	To what extent is the agency realized in reliance systems being used to undermine the natural foundations of these systems?
6 Transparency	To what degree are the terms of the deal knowable to all parties?	To what degree are the terms of the deal obscured?

transgresses planetary boundaries. This is why our use of Sen and Nussbaum is important. How much access is needed for capabilities to be realized? How much access is enough before the freedom of one reduces the freedom of another? Integrating planetary boundaries does mean either some form of technological substitution or change to consumption patterns in much of the developed world to make and remake healthy spatial contracts.

These principles also serve as the foundation for an analytical framework which we argue is essential to building a healthier spatial contract rooted in actual systems, not in political ideology. The next step in this process is to understand systems on their own terms, a process we call 'seeing like a system'.

Notes

1 See I. Berlin, 'Two concepts of liberty', in *Four Essays on Liberty* (Oxford: Oxford University Press, 1969), pp. 118–72. Berlin famously developed his concept of negative liberty alongside a concept of 'positive liberty', which he argued was what concerned theorists such as Rousseau and Hegel. Positive liberty for Berlin is the psychological capacity to settle authentically how you are going to live. Berlin judged the latter form of freedom to be insidious. The former sort of freedom – negative freedom – was judged to be more attractive.

2 See G. A. Cohen, 'Are disadvantaged workers who take hazardous jobs forced to take hazardous jobs?', in G. A. Cohen, *History, Labour, and Freedom* (Oxford: Clarendon Press, 1988), pp. 239–54.

3 Even quite sophisticated accounts of republican freedom are built around thinking about freedom in terms of absences. See P. Petit, *A Theory of Freedom* (Cambridge: Polity, 2001).

4 Historically, the modern concept of freedom was often cashed out by contrasting it with the condition of the slave. One is free, on this view, when one is not a slave, which is just to say that one is free when one is not unfree. A good overview of this tradition in the American context is A. Rana, *The Two Faces of*

American Freedom (Cambridge, MA: Harvard University Press, 2014).

5 K. Marx and F. Engels, *The German Ideology*, in *Collected Works*, vol. 5 (London: Lawrence and Wishart, 1976), p. 394, cited in G. A. Cohen, 'Reconsidering historical materialism', *Nomos* 26 (1983), pp. 227–51 (pp. 248–9).

6 K. Marx and F. Engels, 'The Holy Family', in *Collected Works*, vol. 4 (London: Lawrence and Wishart, 2010), p. 131. We can put aside any objections to or observations about the excesses of Marx's own materialist approach to freedom and still appreciate how different this is from the purely negative understanding of freedom. See G. A. Cohen, *Karl Marx's Theory of History: A Defence* (Princeton, NJ: Princeton University Press, 1979), ch. 4.

7 See J. Rawls, *A Theory of Justice* (Cambridge, MA: Belknap Press of Harvard University Press, 1971).

8 See A. Sen, 'Equality of what?', in S. McMurrin (ed.), *Tanner Lectures on Human Values*, vol. 1 (Cambridge: Cambridge University Press, 1980), pp. 195–220.

9 For example, Sen writes: 'Variations in environmental conditions ... can influence what a person gets out of a given level of income. Heating and clothing requirements of the poor in colder climates cause problems that may not be shared by equally poor people in warmer lands. The presence of infectious diseases in a region ... alters the quality of life that inhabitants of that region may enjoy.' A. Sen, *Development as Freedom* (New York: Oxford University Press, 1999), p. 70.

10 Consider Rawls's two principles of justice (see Rawls, *A Theory of Justice*, pp. 52–6, for their introduction) which are distinct and ordered, such that trade-offs between the second (governing the distribution of opportunities and resources) and the first (governing the distribution of freedoms) are not permitted. For Rawls, at least, restricting certain civil rights for the sake of increases in the level of resources gained by the least well-off (relative to resource distribution) is in principle objectionable. There may be a strong correlation, of course, between improvements in civil freedoms and improvements in the distributive shares going to the least well-off. But that *empirical* relationship is not Rawls's justification for the ordering of the principles of justice. Rather, he argues that *in principle* rational agents

behind a veil of ignorance would reject such trade because liberty has priority *in principle* over resource distribution.

11 This is bold because it seems to take an illiberal stand on what counts as a good life or a life worth living. However, Sen thinks that we cannot avoid making some sort of claim about that. And if we focus on basic capabilities, then the objection loses some of its bite.

12 There is a vast literature on this topic. The best, albeit slightly dated, overview with ample citations is S. Alkire, *Valuing Freedoms: Sen's Capability Approach and Poverty Reduction* (New York: Oxford University Press, 2002).

13 More specifically, 'the capability is a set of such functioning n-tuples, representing the various combination of beings and doings any one (combination) of which the person can choose. Capability is thus defined in the *space* of functionings. If a functioning achievement (in the form of an n-tuple of function-ings) is a *point* in that space, capability is a *set* of such points (representing the alternative functioning tuples from which one n-tuple can be chosen.' A. Sen, 'Capability and well-being', in M. Nussbaum and A. Sen, *The Quality of Life* (Oxford: Clarendon Press, 1993), pp. 30–53 (p. 38). And: 'if the achieved functionings constitute a person's well-being, then the capability to achieve functionings (i.e., all the alternative combinations of functionings a person can choose to have) will constitute the person's freedom – the real opportunities – to have well-being'. A. Sen, *Inequality Re-examined* (Cambridge, MA: Harvard University Press, 1995), p. 40.

14 Sen, 'Capability and well-being', p. 31.

15 Sen writes of Rawls's primary goods, Ronald Dworkin's account of resources as the metric of equality, and familiar macro-economic metrics such as GNP and GDP that they are 'concerned [only] with the instruments of achieving well-being and other objectives, and can be seen as the means to freedom. In contrast, functionings belong to the constitutive elements of well-being. Capability reflects freedom to pursue these constitutive elements, and may even have … a direct role in well-being itself, in so far as deciding and choosing are also parts of living'. Sen, *Inequality Re-examined*, p. 42. In *Development as Freedom*, p. 74, Sen writes that the 'space' over which distributive justice operates 'is neither that of utilities (as claimed by welfarists), nor that of

primary goods (as demanded by Rawls), but that of the substantive freedoms – the capabilities – to choose a life one has reason to value'. As is clear, Sen treats capability space as defining not just freedom but also the space in which well-being – in the form of a set of functionings – is realized.

16 For a classic essay in political theory critiquing models of negative liberty along related lines, see J. Waldron, 'Homelessness and the issue of freedom', *UCLA Law Review* 39 (1991–92), pp. 295–324 (p. 295).

17 M. Nussbaum, *Creating Capabilities: The Human Development Approach* (Cambridge, MA: Belknap Press of Harvard University Press, 2011), p. 18. Nussbaum initially referred to capabilities as 'capacities'. This was because of the Aristotelian foundations of her approach. Aristotle defined biological organisms in terms of their 'potentialities'. Nussbaum eventually joined Sen in using the term 'capabilities'.

18 Ibid. Nussbaum's departure from Sen is in her proposal of central capabilities. These are, she thinks, to be construed as universal (relative to humans). Sen, on the other hand, has argued that the capabilities that a society ought to produce and respect are subject to democratic selection. This is a difficult issue that we do not address, even if we recognize that resolving it cannot be put off indefinitely.

19 It immediately becomes clear that capabilities are always qualified: X is capable of F-ing *without undue burden*. So, for example, someone may be able to express a political opinion, but with the expectation that she will suffer horrible consequences (ostracism, prison, beatings or even death). To say that this person lacks the capability to express certain political opinions – that this person is not free to express certain political opinions – is just shorthand for saying that this person lacks the capability of expressing certain political opinions *without the credible fear of serious reprisals*. This is the shorthand we will use.

20 This fits with a long tradition in the philosophy of agency in which a philosopher's paradigm of human agency is typically the trivial capacity to raise one's arm. A fine summary of this view is offered by the contemporary philosopher Michael Smith, who writes: 'Actions are those bodily movements that are caused and rationalized by a pair of mental states: a desire for some end, where ends can be thought of as ways the world could be, and

a belief that something the agent can just do, namely, move her body in the way to be explained, has some suitable chance of making the world the relevant way.' M. Smith, 'The structure of orthonomy', in J. Hyman and H. Steward (eds), *Agency and Actions* (Cambridge: Cambridge University Press, 2004), pp. 165–93 (p. 165). See also M. Smith, 'Four objections to the standard story of action (and four replies)', *Philosophical Issues* 22 (2012), pp. 387–401, esp. pp. 396ff.

21 This list is from Sen, *Inequality Re-examined*, p. 40.

22 We find similar views expressed in disability studies. See, for example, G. L. Albrecht (ed.), *Handbook of Disability Studies* (Thousand Oaks, CA: Sage, 2001), especially D. Wasserman, 'Philosophical issues in the definition and social response to disability', pp. 219–51; and S. Tremain, 'On the government of disability', *Social Theory and Practice* 27 (2001), pp. 617–36 (p. 617).

23 This omission is understandable, as the intellectual history of the development of the capabilities approach has always placed the focus on questions of choice, freedom, welfare and justice. But it is still a lacuna, since they are also explicit in making human agency – the capacity for human beings to act – the focus of their politics.

24 How free someone is depends on what agential capacities they have. The more agential capacities a person has, the freer they are. But the capacity to act is not the same as taking an action. A person can have the capacity to ride a bicycle because they own a bicycle or could easily buy a bicycle, and they live in an area that is conducive to riding a bicycle. Yet they never ride a bicycle. In this way, people are often free to take actions that they never take. This is the sort of freedom – the sort of agential capacity – realized in reliance systems.

25 Some interesting defences of views along these lines can be found in legal scholarship. See, for example, N. K. Katyal, 'Architecture as crime control', *Yale Law Journal* 111 (2002), pp. 1039–139; L. Tien, 'Architectural regulation and the evolution of social norms', *Yale Journal of Law and Technology* 7 (2004–05), pp. 1–22; S. Schindler, 'Architectural exclusion, discrimination and segregation through physical design of the built environment', *Yale Law Journal* 124 (2014–15), pp. 1934–2024.

26 We shall often refer to reliance systems by reference to some artefact, in the same way that we might refer to a piece of music by referring to its score. For example, we refer to the reliance system re/producing subway infrastructure as the subway, or the reliance system re/producing energy infrastructure as the energy grid, but this is shorthand.

27 See L. Björkman, *Pipe Politics, Contested Waters: Embedded Structures of Millennial Mumbai* (Durham, NC: Duke University Press, 2015).

28 We do not intend this as a definitive breakdown of reliance systems. For further analysis of reliance systems, see Smith, 'Reliance structures: how urban public policy shapes human agency'.

29 Recall that the material component is really a system and we are using the terms 'strip of asphalt' and 'painted lanes' to refer to the systems that re/produce these things.

30 One might argue that this engagement with each other is facilitated by the state or the market. Why not then simply employ familiar theories of the state or the market? The spaces in which the engagement occurs are themselves constantly transforming. They also are (in part) material systems. The Athenian assembly could not function without a place in which the citizens met. This place had to have the sorts of acoustics that allowed for speeches and debate. Such a space had to be built. The same point applies today. We cannot, then, think entirely abstractly about the role that the market or the state plays in facilitating settlements governing the production of reliance systems. This is why a spatial contract and not a social contract is required.

31 We discuss this need in the conclusion.

32 We leave aside epistemic accounts of democracy, according to which governance is legitimate when, through democratic means, it arrives at the correct policy. See D. Estlund, *Democratic Authority* (Princeton, NJ: Princeton University Press, 2007).

33 J. Elster, 'The market and the forum: three varieties of political theory', in J. Elster and A. Hylland (eds), *Foundations of Social Choice Theory* (Cambridge: Cambridge University Press, 1986), pp. 103–32 (p. 122).

34 J. Bohman, 'The coming of age of deliberative democracy', *Journal of Political Philosophy* 4 (1998), pp. 400–25 (p. 401).

35 On public spheres, the key figure is, of course, Jürgen Habermas. The central idea is that in such publics, 'no force except that of the better argument is exercised'. J. Habermas, *Legitimation Crisis*, trans. T. McCarthy (New York: Polity, 1976), p. 108.

36 J. Cohen, 'Deliberation and democratic legitimacy', in A. Hamlin and P. Petit (eds), *The Good Polity: Normative Analysis of the State* (Oxford: Basil Blackwell, 1989), p. 21.

37 S. Benhabib, *Situating the Self* (New York: Routledge, 1992), p. 9.

38 J. Elster, 'Deliberation and constitution making', in J. Elster (ed.), *Deliberative Democracy* (Cambridge: Cambridge University Press, 1998), pp. 97–122 (p. 111). For challenges and complications to this view, see J. Mansbridge et al., 'The place of self-interest and the role of power in deliberative democracy', *Journal of Political Philosophy* 1 (2010), pp. 64–100.

39 Rawls acknowledges the significance of the material in the second principle of justice. This principle deals with non-juridical forms of inequality, characterized in terms of departures from equal distributions of baskets of what Rawls calls primary goods. But, curiously, Rawls does not characterize primary goods in explicitly material terms beyond the category of income and wealth. As a result, the second principle of justice is blind to the material constitution of human life.

40 For example, the telephone infrastructure can be recruited to realize the capacity of using the internet while remaining a reliance system for telephonic communication; a postal system can be increasingly recruited for realizing the aim of shopping for commodities while remaining a reliance system for private communication; and so on.

41 United Nations Food and Agriculture Organization, *Status of the World's Soils, Main Report* (Rome: FAO, 2015).

42 J. Rockström et al. 'Planetary boundaries: exploring the safe operating space for humanity', *Ecology and Society* 14.2 (2009).

43 We recognize that the concept of transparency has often been used by international agencies as a means of promoting certain regimes of development which violate both this principle and others. See, for instance, H. Kim, 'Capturing world class urbanism through modal governance in Saigon', *positions: asia critique* 25.4 (2017), pp. 669–92.

2 Seeing like a system

Thus far, we have worked to establish two critical points. First, human freedom is realized in reliance systems, social and material systems that have to be constantly made and remade. These systems, no matter our individual capacities, are always collectively produced. Second, these reliance systems are governed by a set of formal and informal political agreements which we call spatial contracts. Spatial contracts are *spatial* and not exclusively social because they are rooted in the materiality of specific systems, and thus in both space, place and time. There are no reliance systems that exist outside of history and geography.

These two points form the foundation of this book's *intellectual framework*. The next step is to develop a clearer way of analysing any given spatial contract. We started this process of developing an *analytical framework* in the previous chapter by introducing a set of six principles aimed at helping analyse the underlying morality of any given spatial contract. To us, questions of purpose, system strength, access and inclusion, exploitation and oppression, planetary boundaries and transparency must be at the heart of any morally acceptable analysis of spatial contracts.

Further developing this analytical framework is the primary task of this chapter and the two that follow. This chapter focuses on one of the most challenging components of spatial contracts and reliance systems: the material, historical and geographical specificity of each system. How do we understand systems on their own terms? How do we avoid universalizing ideologies, and instead learn to pull apart given systems to understand how they operate? How do we, in the language of this chapter's title, learn to 'see like a system'?

The starting point for analysing spatial contracts is to begin with reliance systems *as they are*, often beginning with simple questions. Where does our water come from? How does the system work? Who is paying and how? This means starting from the system and building a politics from that point, what we think of as a 'system-centred' understanding of politics, as opposed to a 'politics-centred' understanding of the system.[1] We need a much richer understanding of reliance systems if we are to build a new politics around them, without necessarily becoming experts in all of these systems. We need to change our perspective, understand how they are made, understand the terms of the deal, and put them in their historical, technical and social contexts. This is what we mean by 'seeing like a system'.

We build this framework by drawing on ideas from a diverse set of academic fields, and doing so in a very deliberate, two-step process. We begin with ideas drawn from systems thinking, sketching out ways in which systems are dynamic and ever-changing, and how they are both social and technical in nature. We then add in three important ideas from different corners of systems thinking: the way in which context and incumbency play a role in understanding existing regimes of provision; the importance of a vertical systems of provision approach, as opposed to exclusively horizontal approaches that cut across different systems; and the need to incorporate ideas of ecological limits.

This first part of our framework enables us to see reliance systems as systems, as opposed to commodities or objects or outputs, a common way of seeing in economics. Then we reimagine ideas familiar to economists such as substitutability, excludability and rivalry through the lens of systems thinking, as opposed to the commodity-focused approach from mainstream economics. Not only do we work to detach these ideas from commodity-focused imaginations, we also use these ideas to show the limits of ideologies attached to institutional type and scale.

Finally, we bring the two parts together in a series of questions which offer an initial – and partial – analytical framework. The framework allows us to analyse and pull apart systems using a series of simple questions, so that a healthier spatial contract can be built from the system up, not downwards from fixed political or economic ideologies.

Part one: systems thinking

A half century of thinking about systems provides a useful initial foundation for our analytical framework. As a starting point, we weave together five key points from the literature, points that touch on the dynamism of systems, their inherent 'socio-technical' nature, the role of context and incumbency, the importance of seeing systems in a vertical fashion, and the critical importance of ecological limits. While each point below is important – and more lessons could be drawn from other corners of the systems literature – the most vital aspect of this section is to firmly establish the importance of seeing like a system. This becomes even clearer in part two, when we repurpose ideas from economics by reinterpreting them from a commodities-centred perspective to one that sees the full system.

Reliance systems are dynamic and ever-changing

Systems are never in stasis.[2] They are inherently dynamic, even if they seem quite stable (when they are working well). No matter how well the system is built, it always requires maintenance and the constant addition of natural resources, labour and capital. Parts wear out. Things break. If we are talking about relatively stable systems such as housing, we still need to maintain and repair the dwellings, which requires a steady supply of various different parts (all of which are produced in their own systems) and skilled and available labour. If we are talking about more dynamic systems such as food, then the system needs to be effectively reproduced all the time. Fields must be planted and harvested and cleared and fertilized every year if not more often, with equally dynamic systems for distribution, consumption and disposal.

Systems are always open to influence. This means that outside forces can interrupt well-functioning systems, even if internal forces are working perfectly. A natural disaster is the most obvious of these influencers. Political changes, financial market crises, corporate buyouts and takeovers, war, changes in culture or taste or preference – the list of how external factors can influence systems is long. These forces can destabilize or stabilize systems, but external influence is a given.

Perhaps the best way of thinking about systems is that they constantly have to be remade. Virtually all of our reliance systems need to be constantly *reproduced*, no matter how well designed they are, no matter how stable we think they may be. Understanding a spatial contract means grappling with this fact and developing a political economy that can support a healthy reproduction of core systems.

Reliance systems are social and technical systems
Virtually all humans rely on some sort of collective system for the provision of water.[3] The most basic involve taking the water directly from streams or rivers with buckets or jugs, or perhaps from a well, and using it without filtration. The most complex involve hundreds if not thousands of kilometres of piping of different gauges, reservoirs, canals, pumping stations, filtration plants and water companies, rules and regulations and debates about riparian rights.

Especially when you live in a complex system, it is tempting to focus on all of that machinery and piping. We could all do more to appreciate the technical marvel of New York's water system, or the storm sewers of Mendoza in Argentina, which harvest rainfall to water green spaces and urban trees. But a water system is always a mix of people, ideas and objects.

A water system is often visible as technical objects such as pipes, pumps, reservoirs, storm drains, taps and so on, but it is also made, maintained and changed by us. Our collective behaviours and expectations, our cultural preferences, the competence of our water engineers or people involved in water governance, and the condition of materials making up that system all determine whether the system realizes the capacity to do things with water.

This is true regardless of how complex the system is. Cultural norms can play a role in who is involved in obtaining water, whether the water comes from a well or a local stream or a pumping station far away. Which uses get priority when water is limited is generally a result of historical context and who was in power when the system was designed. Who has an enforceable right to water depends on the legal and political culture of the place. Even seemingly scientific facts regarding what counts as clean water are not entirely a matter of science.[4]

Nonetheless, water is still composed of two hydrogen molecules and one oxygen molecule. It still follows the rules of gravity, and has an incredible capacity to absorb any number of chemicals and compounds and host any number of harmful bacteria and amoebae, none of which care about your cultural preferences. When it moves too fast, it can scour pipes, overspill or destroy much of what stands in its way. Buildings more than six storeys in height generally need water tanks on the roof because the standard pressure from pumping stations is not enough to get the water more than 60 feet up in the air. Water tanks or pipes that are built with the wrong materials will leach harmful chemicals into the water.

It follows that a neighbourhood in northern England composed of tightly packed terraced houses has a radically different reliance system to realize the capacity to drink than a neighbourhood of high-rise apartments in Mumbai, to say nothing of the vast differences in the governmentalities regulating these reliance systems.[5] The technical and cultural aspects of reliance systems feedback on one another in an iterative fashion, and we cannot fruitfully untangle technical standards from cultural practices entirely.

At the same time it is important to draw system boundaries to do spatial contract work. We recognize along with Donella Meadows that system boundaries are only inventions; there is no defensible boundary to most systems, and system boundaries rarely respect geographical administration or academic discipline.[6] At the same time it is necessary to place boundaries on a given system in order to explore and change it. Draw a boundary too small and the system will appear completely arbitrary; too large and it is ungovernable. What we are proposing is an approach that starts by recognizing that reliance system are socio-technical, and adding some useful ideas from economics and consumption studies that we then bind into an analytical framework that concludes this chapter.

Context and incumbency
Seeing systems as social and technical helps us understand the diverse ways in which systems do or do not come to be, and how they are or are not maintained. If a healthier spatial contract is needed, for example one that deals with the climate change impacts of a given system, then the solution or solutions will differ given the time- and place-specific nature of each system. Consider the historical case of Dutch sewers. The Dutch are considered among the greatest water engineers, and have been for centuries. So why did the construction of sewerage systems in Dutch cities come much later than in other European cities? First, the technical side. The flat topography of the Netherlands meant that gravity-based systems were unsuitable, and more expensive pump-aided infrastructure was needed. Dutch soils were more unstable, meaning that pipe and tunnel subsidence was more likely. Yet both of these factors could have been overcome.

It is only when you add in the political that it makes sense. This extra expense meant that the local governments of the Netherlands resisted change as opposed to leading it. Changes to systems of sewerage provision, away from barrel and pit methods and towards the brick-lined infrastructure and centralized sewage works of London, Paris and other capitals, were only made in the Netherlands after a social movement beyond the city councils emerged to demand change. A mixed profession group, led by hygienists and engineers, used Pasteur's micro-organism theory to give a powerful explanatory narrative to the already proven medical statistics on sanitary conditions and infectious disease. While in other European capitals the statistical relationship between networked sewers and the decreased incidence of infectious disease had been enough to force change, it was Pasteur's explanation of *why* that statistical relation existed, and the social pressure mobilized because of it, that finally broke the resistance of the Dutch city authorities to brick-lined, networked sewerage systems.[7]

This struggle is an example of the process by which a healthier spatial contract is constructed, at least with respect to the capacity to remove waste. This was not a generic social change, but rather a specific, material change in a specific human settlement brought about by a specific interaction between social, material and biological forces. Without a socio-technical systems account, we would be unable to see what it was that finally forced change from one reliance system (barrel and pit methods) to another (the networked sewer model), and changed the spatial contract around sewerage from one form to another in that place at that time.

As with Dutch sewers, new technologies and new systems are almost always grafted on to existing political structures, places and systems. While the technologies may change, while the types of freedoms that are created change, the basic categories of systems are older and more constant. CCTV may have changed policing, but policing is very old. Nano-machines may change medicine, as germ theory did a century ago, but in both cases these were retrofits of existing systems.

In socio-technical systems circles, these various forces for and against change have been characterized in the 'multi-level perspective' popularized by the academic Frank Geels. In the multi-level perspective, broad societal/cultural/ecological changes that affect discrete reliance systems operate as 'landscape' factors, the existing system of provision and its institutions are known as the 'regime', and small-scale disruptors, whether technical, social or commercial, are known as 'niches'. The 'regime' is a representation of what currently is: it is the mix of technologies, institutions, politics, practices and so on that have ossified around a more or less stable spatial contract. Purposive changes to this regime require a new settlement, a new contractual relation that may change one or several parts of the regime.

To see reliance systems as dynamic is to see the wealth of influences on them, the volume and velocity of change pressures acting on them. To see reliance systems as socio-technical is to begin to categorize this dynamism into discrete elements, as subsystems that co-evolve with one another, affecting the direction or stability of the regime through time. As each element of the system evolves, changes in technology can affect all parts of a given system and vice versa.[8]

If a system is dynamic, then how do regimes endure? How does one spatial contract last for any length of time? The answer is that they all have different timescales and different levels of *incumbency*. For example, prior to 1990 the UK energy system was a state-owned *regime* reliant on coal-generation technology for large, centralized power plants. A party-political change that ideologically favoured privatization and free markets led to an intentional change to the institutions governing the energy system, which in turn allowed a niche of private companies to enter the market. Subsequently the private companies aimed their business strategies at natural gas generation (because of the resources in the North Sea), changing the technologies of electricity provision. As a result, prices dropped. This in turn affected user practices. The spatial contract around electricity was fundamentally remade. The dominant state regime gave way to a private regime of utility companies. The transformation had wide effects.

At the time of writing (2019) these companies, the state apparatus of energy market regulation, the mix of gas generation and large renewables, and the normalized practice of consumers choosing an energy supplier are the new regime. However, this regime faces change pressure from small-scale renewables, new digital energy-service providers and new regulations on pollution.

These change pressures are resisted, accommodated, lobbied against or regulated away by the incumbent regime. Incumbents make up a regime at a particular point in time and they are always facing change pressures. The question is how these pressures are dealt with by incumbents. Incumbency is not just the mix of big corporations and state investment. Incumbency includes our own attitudes to, and use of, energy, such as our purchasing habits and home-improvement priorities.

If, for example, the price of solar panels keeps dropping, then it makes more and more sense for homeowners to install solar systems. The more panels, the more solar power on the wider electricity system; but this fluctuates when the sun goes in or comes out. This does not just take money away from utilities that previously provided the electricity, it also impacts the very technological foundations of a system that was designed to run within set frequency limits. On a very sunny day with patchy cloud cover, this can play havoc with the electricity grid; on a longer timescale it means that new grid rules need to be written (institutions), new technologies need to be added to balance power on the system, new balancing businesses emerge (business strategies) and, ultimately, ecosystems change relative to the greenhouse gas reductions that result from using more solar power. In terms of the spatial contract, what is happening? A new element is introduced, and this has effects across the regime. As a result, it challenges incumbency. This forces a change to the regime, and a change to the existing spatial contract.

We then need to ask what this actually means in terms of the principles of a 'healthy' spatial contract. The electricity may be 'greener', but who is paying the subsidies for the solar power? Are the fuel-poor being disadvantaged? Whose voices are heard and not heard in deciding where solar farms are built?

The socio-technical systems field is good for seeing the system, but it provides little in the way of describing the specifics of consumption in a particular place. For that we require a framework that brings in a more explicitly vertical political economy, one that can see what consumption capacities are realized by what types of provision, and track who is doing what at which points in the supply chain.

Reliance systems as systems of provision

The socio-technical systems approach helps us see the human and non-human side of systems, and helps us appreciate that all systems have vital historical, geographical and cultural context. But more is needed to understand the difference between water and housing and healthcare. Our approach is heavily informed by the work of the economists Ben Fine and Ellen Leopold, who developed what is known as the 'systems of provision' approach.

Fine and Leopold define 'systems of provision' as a way to understand each commodity as unique 'in terms of a unity of economic and social processes which vary *significantly from one commodity to another*'.[9] Fine developed the systems of provision approach specifically out of frustration with mainstream neoclassical economics, and its assumptions about the way markets behave and the unrealism of the individual as a pleasure-seeking, means/ends-calculating machine; a 'utility maximizer'.[10] For Fine and Leopold, the way mainstream economics treats all markets as derived from a simple relation between supply and demand seemed to ignore the most basic of questions: the economics of what? Housing? Cosmetics?[11]

Too often lost in talk of 'the economy' or debates about 'the state' or 'the market' are the vast difference between commodities. The basic materials of everyday life are exceptionally diverse in their production cycles, their economic

geographies, the complexity of their inputs, their spatial relations and reliance on land, their basic consumer sovereignty.
So, for instance, take two important systems: water and
electricity.[12] We often group these together under the idea of
'services' or 'utilities', but they could not be more different.
Water is both the raw material and the end product, while
electricity can be derived from many different sources, can
be carried by a single infrastructure, cannot be stored and is
recruited for many agential capacities (the capacity to illuminate, the capacity to charge a phone, the capacity to cool a
home, and so on). The cultural imagination of what electricity and water are is different, they are often run by different
institutions, and the electricity system of provision generally
has far more actors and is far more diverse than is water.

Water and electricity require radically different types of
expertise, above and beyond engineering. A healthy water
system is addressed more in terms of biology, a healthy
electricity system more in terms of physics (at least for
the moment). Different inputs, different outputs, different
economies, different cultures, different institutions – that is,
different systems of provision. While some of us might pay a
single major multinational or municipal corporation for both
energy and water, how they get to the point of consumption,
and the freedoms they realize, could not be more different. As
Fine et al. argue,

> Distinctions need to be made not only in their material proper-
> ties and meanings to consumers, but also in how they are pro-
> vided. In a nutshell, energy, housing, fashion and food systems
> are all distinctive by virtue of the structures, relations, pro-
> cesses and agencies of provision of which they are comprised.[13]

When we start to see things *vertically*, that is, from the beginning of a system and all its inputs to the ultimate point of
consumption, and indeed the human agency that consumption realizes, we can start to develop analytical tools that help
us identify key differences in systems. Beginning as it did in

consumption studies, the systems of provision approach has often been applied to consumer commodities such as clothing or milk. But we can also take the vertical approach to systems such as water. This allow us to draw a cartography of provision from consumption right up through corporate ownership and operative structures. This reveals how and why water provision in England is so beholden to the needs of global finance. It allows us to speculate in detail as to why this does not cause far more of a social outcry, as it would probably do if this model were deployed elsewhere in the world.[14]

This vertical, commodity-specific political economy is hugely important, as it animates and defines the socio-technical systems account, which at times is apolitical. Where the socio-technical systems field allows us to see like a system, applying a systems of provision approach allows us to see who wins and who loses, who is being exploited and why, what cultural meanings are at work, and which horizontal processes, such as financialization, nationalism and so on, are having direct influence on the existing regime.[15] By taking consumption as seriously as production, it enables us to see the full life cycle of reliance systems.

What does this mean for understanding the spatial contract? Take the case of the capacity to warm oneself. In any latitude outside the tropics, this requires a heating system. These systems often constitute other capacities such as the capacity to dry clothes, the capacity to bathe in hot water and so on (depending upon one's heating system). Surely the most efficient, cheapest and most environmentally beneficial heat source would be required for a healthy spatial contract?

In some cases this would mean building heat networks, in which centrally generated heat is delivered to multiple homes. It is a common feature across northern Europe and Scandinavia, and if done correctly, can have substantial efficiency benefits. A compelling case has been made for the expansion of heat networks in the United Kingdom, where in spite of a milder climate, more people live in fuel poverty than in Scandinavian countries.[16] However, cultural meanings of consumption matter, and historical providers matter. In one study, regardless of the economic and health benefits, UK consumers were seen as reluctant to adopt this technology due to its prior association with council housing. It was deemed 'poor man's heating' and faces several culturally constructed barriers to adoption.[17]

The systems of provision approach asks us to consider who is responsible for providing what, and the ways in which the organization of provision affects consumption and the cultural meaning of individual commodities. If this is extended to reliance systems, as opposed to individual commodities, we are invited to ask not only socio-technical questions about technologies, user practices, institutions and regimes, but what these *mean* in a specific place or time.

What does it *mean* to cycle in a city? Cycling is becoming a more legitimate means of mobility for the middle classes in India.[18] In turn this opens new territory for a spatial contract around urban mobility infrastructure which includes safe cycling.[19] This may be true for a salaried middle class in Bangalore, but it sometimes depends on consuming high-end cycling equipment to distinguish oneself from the poor. Imported high-end bikes are particularly useful as class signifiers because they are so much more expensive than domestic, low-tech cycles. India struggles to build a mid-section of the cycling economy because mid-section bikes are usually based on aluminium components. India has aluminium production facilities but not secondary aluminium fabrication facilities. This makes imported high-end bicycles all the more of a cultural distinguisher of a salaried white-collar worker; access to *this* cycling culture is closely restricted.[20] At first sight, Bangalore's bucking of the trend of declining cycling rates in India might suggest that the spatial contract on mobility in that place is becoming healthier. But is this really an improvement if it relies on class exclusion and othering of the poor? Whose voices are being heard here in urban planning, and how do these cultural meanings affect which cycle lanes get built, who they are for and how they are maintained?[21] How does cultural meaning inform a new spatial contract for bicycle-based mobility in Bangalore? The socio-technical systems field would miss this, where a systems of provision account would not. A healthy spatial contract would be responsive to all of this.

Reliance systems as ecological systems

One of our key principles for a healthy spatial contract is that it respects planetary boundaries. These are ecological limits to resource extraction, or waste sinks; crossing planetary boundaries begins to lock in hugely damaging practices that will lead to ecological crises.[22] The reason we cross these planetary boundaries is largely due to the unhealthy spatial contracts we have created to provision reliance systems.

Reliance systems are material. To cook with natural gas we need to drill for it or fracture it right out of the rock. To create a road we need to quarry rock, to build a tower we need to manufacture concrete, to nourish a cow to get meat or milk we need pasture or feed. For most of the Global North, the production and reproduction of reliance systems takes us well beyond planetary boundaries. For much of the Global South, provision of reliance systems remains well within planetary boundaries, but many fewer capacities are produced.[23]

Every reliance system processes energy and matter at different rates. Provisioning human freedoms while respecting planetary boundaries is extremely difficult. It is system-specific, so to think about ecological solutions in terms of an abstract, broad, 'new social contract' is extremely difficult. Calls for a 'new social contract' are searching for a generalized politics which replicates a settlement between capital and labour but with ecological sensibilities, a 'green new deal'.[24] The sentiment here is laudable, but in practice any green new deal will have to deal with the material specificity of existing reliance systems; it will have to work system by system, place by place. It would mean entering people's homes to retrofit energy efficiency; it would mean material changes to commuting patterns, dietary changes and land reform.

Seeing like a system, understanding systems of provision and contending with ecological crises means building spatial contracts that are deeply disruptive for existing sociotechnical *regimes*. This disruption will mean reallocation of costs, benefits, consumption levels, ownership and control, as well as the addition of new technologies and cultural meaning.

Because the construction of new spatial contracts will inevitably contend with the allocation of scarce resources, we need one additional framework to understand how this allocation is best discussed, and for this we tentatively approach mainstream economics.

Part two: repurposing economics

The systems approaches in part one of this chapter provide a foundation for system-centric thinking. The next step is to incorporate ideas from mainstream economics, with some caution, as these ideas need to be adapted to be useful in a spatial contract sense. We focus on two concepts, one from the world of consumer-choice economics, the other from public goods theory, both of which can be very useful if they are adapted from a commodity-centred perspective to a more systems-centred one.[25] We then highlight how ideology, from various corners of political economy, can fixate on certain sectors, institution or scales as somehow inherently ideal for systems of provision. Stepping away from these ideological approaches is central to seeing like a system.

Substitutability
Substitutability is a concept that emerges from the economics of consumption. Substitutability asks whether one can successfully substitute one product for another. If there is a shortage of tea, or the price of tea goes up, will people switch to coffee? If the price of oil goes up, can people switch to gas?

In mainstream economics, substitutability as a concept is designed to understand elasticity, that is, how one economic variable responds to another. It has an opposite in 'complementarity', the extent to which demand for one good drives demand for another. The classic textbook example is that if you produce hamburgers, this will drive demand for soft drinks, condiments, buns, etc. Mainstream economics cares about tea and coffee because they believe that if the price of one goes up, people will switch.

Mainstream economics thinks in terms of commodities, not systems, so it doesn't see the full socio-technical system of provision which we argue is necessary. If we see things as a system, this isn't so easy. Yes, butter and margarine, which are classic textbook examples of substitutability, can be easily interchanged – but only if people eat dairy. Oil and gas both provide energy, but good luck burning gas in your oil heater; you might be able to burn hydrogen in your gas heater, but your existing legacy infrastructure will define the mix that is safe. An incumbent gas firm might push hydrogen solutions because they are compatible with their existing business model of providing a fuel to burn at home through pipes, but retrofitting homes with electric heating or the aforementioned heat networks may have much better economic and environmental outcomes.

When you are interested in systems of provision, as we are, and not theoretical supply and demand relationships, what is substitutable and what is not changes. Grains tend to be very substitutable at the point of consumption – most humans can digest most grains, and few cultures have taboos on specific grain consumption.[26] But grains are not inherently substitutable when it comes to growing them. That requires specific soils, climates, techniques and so on.

Thus, while the concept of substitutability is vital for systems thinking, it must be adapted from mainstream economics to a system-approach which sees the bigger picture. The electrical system has a high degree of substitutability at certain points in the system – once you convert something into electricity, the electrical grid is happy to accept it.[27] But if you run out of coal, or ban it, converting your power plant to run on something else is expensive, time-consuming, politically and even culturally complex.[28]

A commodity-centred perspective fails to prepare us for inevitable changes in the system, changes that go beyond consumer preferences, demand and supply. Demand for electricity doesn't drop during a hurricane – it is the system that fails. Demand for housing doesn't drop during an economic crisis, simply the ability to access this system under current rules. A systems perspective forces a re-evaluation of what is really substitutable for what when provisioning human freedoms.

Are reliance systems public goods?

Another set of concepts from mainstream economics refers not to questions of demand and elasticity, but to basic material questions of access to economic goods. The first idea is the notion of excludability, that is, the extent to which someone can be excluded from a particular commodity or system for any reason. It is relatively easy to keep someone out of a cinema if they don't have a ticket, almost impossible to prevent someone from breathing clean air if the air around them is clean. Thus clean air is considered non-excludable, and the cinema is considered excludable.

The second notion is rivalry, which is the degree to which consumption by one person or community prevents simultaneous consumption by another. So, for instance, radio programmes are classic examples of non-rivalrous goods, since it doesn't matter how many people are listening to the radio. One more listener changes nothing. Cars, and most other durable goods, are rivalrous. One person's use of the car generally makes it hard for others to use it at the same time.

Rivalry and excludability are almost as foundational to the teaching of mainstream economics as supply and demand, and are generally rendered in a famous 2 x 2 table. Something like a car is both excludable and rivalrous, while something like national defence can be consumed by everyone at the

Table 2.1   Traditional understandings of excludability and rivalry

Principle	Excludable	Non-excludable
Rivalrous	Cars, pans, haircuts	Fish stocks, forests, irrigation systems
Non-rivalrous	Satellite television, private parks, car clubs	National defence, public safety, emergency services, roads

same time without a problem, and it is almost impossible to exclude someone.

The challenge from a systems perspective is twofold. First, as with substitutability, mainstream economics considers only the final product, not the system as a whole. Just because radio programming is non-rivalrous doesn't do you any good if you don't have access to the rivalrous good that is a radio. While the signal itself is non-excludable within range of a transmitter, this is no good if you are out of range. Furthermore, while radio programming is non-rivalrous, the goods involved in radio production and broadcasting typically are.

A commodity-based perspective is also less sensitive to changes in systems. Technology has changed in ways that make types of exclusion more possible. Take, for instance, roads, our key reliance system from Chapter 1. For a long time they were thought of as non-excludable, but technological advancement, new laws and new norms have made roads more and more excludable. Placing a toll booth with a human being inside to collect revenues is expensive; using digital licence plate capture and automated payment systems is much cheaper. Roads of a certain kind have thus become more excludable. Rising congestion means we question their non-rivalrous nature. Is the road now a private good because it is excludable and rivalrous? *Should* we change the whole way we provide roads because we *can*, or *should* we deal with the congestion problem by seeing the *system* of urban mobility and building some cycle paths instead?

That word *should* is critical; it implies a contested decision. The issue with the 2 x 2 table above is not that it isn't useful, it's that it can be connected ideologically to a certain means of provision. The table above is usually rendered with labels for each box, labels that are at least partly responsible for three separate Nobel Prizes in Economics. Goods that are excludable and rivalrous are talked of as private goods, while non-excludable, non-rivalrous goods are referred to as public goods.[29] The logic in calling them public goods is that their non-rivalrous, non-excludable nature makes it unlikely that the 'market' – that is, private, for-profit institutions – will provide them.

A famous example is a lighthouse.[30] A lighthouse is not rivalrous in consumption, as any number of ships sailing along a coast can use its light without diminishing the ability of other ships to also use that light. It is also non-excludable in that it is very difficult to create a market in which all ships that benefit pay for that benefit. Since it is very difficult to charge ships for using lighthouses, the 'market' is unlikely to provide them. The market has then 'failed' because of the characteristics of lighthouses, and the state should theoretically step in to ensure that lighthouses are provided, because the economic costs of going without them are higher than

Table 2.2 Excludability and rivalry with (Nobel-winning) ideologies

Principle	Excludable	Non-excludable
Rivalrous	**Private goods:** cars, pans, haircuts	**Common-pool resources:** fish stocks, forests, irrigation systems
Non-rivalrous	**Club goods:** satellite television, private parks, car clubs	**Public goods:** National defence, public safety, emergency services, lighthouses

their costs of provision (shipwrecks are expensive and tragic, lighthouses in comparison are cheap). Hence the term 'public good'.

Goods that are excludable but not rivalrous – satellite television for instance – are dubbed 'club goods' for obvious reasons – they can be shared easily, yet one can still be excluded.[31] Club goods are often impacted by congestion, that is, they are generally non-rivalrous to a point, but once there is a critical mass of swimmers in a pool or golfers on the links, rivalry becomes a problem. Since exclusion is possible, fees and other barriers are erected.

The final label is for rivalrous but non-excludable goods, which are deemed 'common-pool resources', a term coined by Vincent and Elinor Ostrom.[32] The classic examples are forests and fish stocks. It is difficult to stop people fishing in the ocean – all you need is a rod, line and boat; but if lots of people want fish and there are only so many fish to go round, the resource pool is subtracted from. You cannot catch the same fish that I just caught, and you cannot catch the same shoal with a trawler that I just caught. This point of congestion is also important because it means that rivalry is not black and white; for many goods there is a point of congestion or over-harvesting that ruins things for everyone.[33]

Duelling ideologies: sectors and scales
Where ideology comes into play is when we assume that a particular system of provision, a certain type of governance structure, automatically works for a certain good. As we have noted, the first problem is that we need to be examining systems, not goods. Fisheries are a system, not simply the output (fish). They change for all the reasons discussed above.

These ideological perspectives generally take two forms: the belief in a certain sector or institutional form (i.e. state vs market vs commons), and the belief in a certain scale (i.e. local, regional, national, global). Rather than seeing excludability and rivalry as useful questions to ask about systems, we have a tendency to use these concepts to attempt to prove that one way of collective provisioning is better.

Take, for instance, the work of Ostrom, which can be interpreted in two ways. On the one hand, the classic textbook understanding is that Ostrom believed in small-to medium-sized, non-state institutions. She is an icon of commons-type approaches, highlighting the power of communal ownership and co-produced rule systems particularly for small/medium-sized natural resource systems, a belief that polycentric governance, cooperation and institution building could effectively manage common-pool resources. This is often contested by those who subscribe to Hardin's 'tragedy of the commons' argument.[34] Hardin used a common grazed pasture example, where more and more commoners add more and more grazing animals until the pasture is exhausted. Hardin argued that this meant that common-pool resources are best protected when higher-level authorities either regulate the resource, or assign and enforce private property rights to prevent over-exploitation.

Yet from a systems perspective, a more useful interpretation of Ostrom comes from what legal scholar Lee Anne Fennell calls Ostrom's Law, the notion that '[a] resource arrangement that works in practice can work in theory'.[35] Ostrom's work was resolutely empirical, attempting to show that for many systems, complex, often mixed and multi-scalar arrangements worked in practice in different parts of the world. Her work was *situated* in the specific place, time, culture and institutional arrangements of the system she was studying. The end result was a recognition that most systems have mixed ownership regimes (i.e. private, public, commons, etc.), and that this is 'neither unusual nor avoidable'.[36] They also often exist at different scales. Using Fennell's examples, the scale at which sheep are maintained and that at which the pasture land is governed may be quite different – the former may be much smaller than the latter. Extraction of energy does not occur at the same scale as distribution of energy. In both cases, mixed scales may occur with mixed ownership structures, and in both cases this mixed version may – or may not – be ideal for the given system in the given place at the given time.[37] Ostrom's work, if read through this lens of a ground-up, systems-centred perspective, offers plenty of evidence that to see like a system we must start with the system, not with preconceived notions of the proper *sector* or the proper *scale*.

By placing reliance systems at the heart of our analysis, we are forced to rethink some of the important tenets of both mainstream and alternative economic thinking. A systems-based approach is deeply pragmatic – a system that produces agency is better than a system that does not, irrespective of the scale at which that system operates, or the particular political economy of that system. Scale and political economy are means to an end.

The challenge to mainstream economics is one that we hope is clear.[38] From neoclassical economics to Austrian-influenced neoliberal or libertarian approaches to socialist economics, different forms of economic thinking have fixated on either the state or the market as the sector that is somehow better equipped to produce what needs to be produced. Attached to these ideologies are often beliefs in big business or small business, the centralized bureaucratic state or the local state, or even regional governmentalities in the case of many foundational systems such as transport or housing or sewerage and water.[39]

This sectoral and scalar fixation has its equivalent in alternative economics, including neo-Marxist viewpoints,[40] different forms of commons-based thinking, and numerous social movements responding to the challenges of privatization and state withdrawal from collective provision. While the evidence is clear that a generation of state rollback in collective provision has allowed many reliance systems to be increasing sources of profit and exploitation,[41] it is a mistake to define collective provision through any particular form of institutional or sectoral organization, and an even bigger mistake to adhere to an institutional ideology. State actors of different scales, for-profit actors of different sizes, non-profit and informal institutions can be involved in ways that are productive, non-exploitative and sustainable.[42]

Evidence for the lack of an ideal institutional structure abounds, mostly through the sins of each sector. While evidence of private, for-profit exploitation is abundant, the track record of state providers is far from ideal, from overly centralized and bureaucratic systems that dramatically under-provisioned, to racist and classist uses of state power, often in collaboration with for-profit institutions. Local governments can become clubs for the elite.[43] Non-profit, collectivist institutions can be just as exclusionary, from Homeowner Associations and gated communities in the United States – some of which incorporate as municipalities – to the ongoing challenges of diversity and exclusion in co-housing,[44] an archetypal institutional ideal in many alternative economic circles.[45] Neither protection from violence nor the perpetuation of violence are in reality the monopoly of the state, regardless of what states may imagine.

Yet the strongest argument against institutional or sectoral ideology – and in favour of the 'non-ideological', systems-up approach we argue for here – is political and practical. A healthier spatial contract demands a better and more effective politics, and cannot be built while progressives are hopelessly divided between statist and collectivist institutional imaginations. Typically, evidence of injustice in collective provisioning of reliance systems is quickly followed up by an argument for 'the commons', the 'welfare state', etc., where what is needed is unity around collective provisioning and the immorality of an unhealthy spatial contract. Certainly state power is often (but not always) central to better provisioning. Key alternative mechanisms that are 'collectively' owned have shown promise in specific places and times, and can be extraordinarily helpful and inspirational.

But when considered across cultures, geographies and moments in history, no amount of evidence can support any overarching ideological position with regard to institutions.

Certain types of institutions may in certain places be more effective at provisioning – state-led housing corporations in one place, micro-entrepreneurs in another – but the complex and unique nature of each system belies any form of a priori political structure. As we have stated repeatedly, rather than derive an idealized political structure and apply it to each system – a form of politics-centred systems thinking – we instead need to focus on the system at hand and develop a systems-centred politics. The specific political economy for each system must derive from the historically and geographically specific reliance system.

'Beware the local trap'
The same is true of scale. 'Localism' has become a very powerful ideology for many progressive thinkers.[46] It is understandable that many alternative thinkers have focused on localizing the spatial contract so that the re/production of reliance systems is an entirely local affair. The duelling forces of financialization and globalization have often negatively disrupted key systems of provision. The current heavily globalized system is wasteful and exploitative. There are surely many reliance systems in many places that could be made more equitable, efficient, resilient and less environmentally damaging if their re/production was more localized. This applies to both the material geography of the goods produced by the system – the actual water that moves, the wheat and the sewerage and the transport – and the institutional geography that controls and manages the system.

Forms of localism have had a profound influence in alternative economic thinking, both for those seeking to return to a form of 'municipal socialism' – whereby cities regain power over these systems – or in more anarchist-collectivist formations such as those which derive from Bookchin's 'libertarian municipalism' or from various 'commons' approaches.[47] These approaches make a similar mistake to the sectoral and institutional approaches. Theirs is often a geography-centred way of thinking, whereby an idealized geography is imagined and then applied to the systems to be governed.

The urban planners Brandon Born and Mark Purcell's trenchant critique of localism shows this with regard to food systems, and is worth quoting at length.

> The local is assumed to be desirable; it is preferred a priori to larger scales. What is desired varies and can include ecological sustainability, social justice, democracy, better nutrition, and food security, freshness, and quality. For example, the local trap assumes that a local-scale food system will be inherently more socially just than a national-scale or global-scale food system.
>
> ... there is nothing inherent about any scale. Local-scale food systems are equally likely to be just or unjust, sustainable or unsustainable, secure or insecure. No matter what its scale, the outcomes produced by a food system are contextual: they depend on the actors and agendas that are empowered by the particular social relations in a given food system.[48]

These outcomes depend, as we have argued, on the specific system itself. Local control of decision making on bicycle and pedestrian travel may make sense, but not for long-distance travel. Energy efficiency retrofits of housing may make sense as a neighbourhood/city-scale effort due to building stock expertise and moderate economies of scale,[49] whereas building and regulating electricity and gas transmission grids and interconnection capacity is generally at least a national-scale undertaking.

As with institutional ideologies, the argument against scalar ideology has a practical side. Regardless of what is 'best' or 'ideal', systems in most geographies have long and deep scalar relationships. In some cases, a major political push to alter the scalar relationship is warranted. But in many others, this a priori scalar assumption is a poor place to start. Better to begin with the existing system in that place and time, and analyse from there.

Like Born and Purcell, we are not arguing that the local scale is not important. The transformation of reliance systems from national to regional, or regional to municipal, may improve the spatial contract governing those systems. But our approach, which we see as integral to a healthier spatial contract, demands a system-centred geography, that is, a geography of governance determined by and dependent on the specific system at a specific time and place. It may be large or small, controlled by actors at different scales, but it is the system itself that should determine its geography.

If we maintain focus on the reliance system, we soon recognize that state, for-profit and non-profit actors operating at different scales are most likely involved in virtually every aspect of provision in most places, especially as we turn towards the more complex reliance systems. Many of our systems of provision are deeply embedded, and while clearly many are undervalued economically, exploited for profit or power relentlessly, inadequate in many locales and so on, no amount of political activity is going to effectuate some form of high modernist bulldozing of foundational systems. Such an approach would be a disaster: imagine the effect on human life that the sudden razing of the electricity grid, clean water supply and sewerage systems would have. The complexity and necessity of these systems belies a page 1 rewrite. Successive retrofits piled on top of one another appear revolutionary in hindsight, but to the impatient reformer this path may be unwelcome. Retrofitting is the only revolution that doesn't threaten people's capacities to lead their lives.[50] A retrofit that furthers a healthier spatial contract starts with seeing like a system.

Putting the analytical framework together

The two parts above can be turned into an analytical framework for analysing systems. As a conclusion to this chapter, Table 2.3 shows a simplified version of this framework.[51]

Table 2.3 A basic analytical framework for seeing like a system

Systems	To what extent is the system more or less static? What are the system boundaries? Which change pressures are operating on the system at present?
Socio-technical	What is the current regime composed of? Which technologies, structures, institutions, user practices and business models are in play? What human and ecological effects do they have? What barriers are there to access? What kind of niche innovation might destabilize the incumbent regime? What kind of change pressures are beyond the control of the regime? How much disruption is necessary to achieve a particular system transition, from one state to another?
Systems of provision	What kind of power relations are in play? How are they used to shape the meaning of consumption? How do meanings of consumption affect what is deemed possible or plausible in terms of systems change? Whose interests are being served by the current system of provision? How are broad global and social trends such as financialization, labour casualization and market ideology affecting a specific system?
Ecological	Does the current regime and system of provision respect planetary boundaries? If every human produced reliance systems in this way would waste sinks be exhausted? Resources over-harvested? What is the sustainable level ofconsumption of key underpinning resources for a given reliance system?

Table 2.3 *continued*

Substitutability	To what degree are inputs into the system substitutable? To what degree is the output of a system a substitutable or non-substitutable input into another system? Can the same agential capacites be realized using different material methods of provision?
Rivalry and excludability	Should we exclude people from a given system because we can? How do arguments about the 'efficiency' of creating markets for as many goods as possible actually affect reliance systems? How can our understanding of the system deal with rivalry? Is substitution possible at a point of congestion?
Sector	What kind of mix of state, market and civil society/commons provision characterizes the current system? Are there any incentives operating on the actors involved that undermine or exploit dependence on reliance systems? What level of profit, if any, is morally acceptable for the provisioning of this reliance system? What form of state control is acceptable? Are there examples where a different organizational or sectoral form could eliminate perverse incentives that weaken a spatial contract?
Scale	How would a change to the scale at which this system is delivered affect each of the six principles of a healthy spatial contract? How is risk and resilience discussed in relation to scale? How can scale hide or export the exploitation of those whose capacities are realized by a reliance system? Is there anything from the socio-technical systems analysis that suggests that a new scale is required or possible?

This framework is a first step in a ground-up understanding of systems, an understanding that can never make a clean break from the types of ideologies we describe, but forces a critical take on them, and the consideration of ideology in the context of one system in a given place and time. Yet ideology is more than an error in thinking – it has deep cultural and political roots that are often connected to space and place. Ideology in this sense is a political barrier to a healthier spatial contract, and it is to the question of political barriers attached to place that we now turn.

Notes

1 By insisting on starting with each system as it is, by starting with what we have, we immediately invite accusations of centrism, a kind of 'third way' approach that remains agnostic on the role of the state, market and commons. But the principles that define a healthy spatial contract are not centrist. Centrism is not revolutionary, and bringing reliance systems back in line with planetary boundaries while at the same time expanding access, and eliminating exploitation, would be revolutionary and disruptive. It would mean many revolutions in many places, disrupting many systems. Equally we do not shy away from identifying broad global trends as critical. A water system might be failing due to privatization and financialization, and neoliberalism might have decimated public transport, but spatial contracts existed for water and mobility under communism, fascism and feudalism as well, and some of those were unhealthy too. So adopting an ideological statist, free market or commons/anarchist position for every spatial contract, and arguing that one of these positions will most likely deliver on all six principles, is naïve. Any time a wholesale nationalization, privatization or 'commoning' agenda is being proposed, for many systems at once, this is an 'ideological', politics-centred understanding of systems.

2 We are deliberately avoiding the work of the similarly named 'systems thinking' school that originates in university business schools and is represented by such seminal publications as

P. M. Senge, 'The fifth discipline, the art and practice of the learning organization', *Performance+ Instruction* 30.5 (1991), p. 37. Recently this school has broken out of a simple focus on making individual organizations more productive, and found a moral and even ecological code. See C. O. Scharmer, *Theory U: Learning from the Future as it Emerges* (Oakland, CA: Berrett-Koehler Publishers, 2009); P. M. Senge, 'Systems thinking for a better world', Aalto Systems Forum 2014, https://www.youtube.com/watch?v=0QtQqZ6Q5-o (accessed 17 October 2019). We adopt a socio-technical systems approach based in innovation systems that focus much more strongly on what we have called reliance systems, that is, the energy system, the sewage system etc., than organizational change. These approaches share *some* common intellectual genealogy, but not much, and it is not productive to explore this here.

3 The socio-technical systems approach owes much to the work of Thomas P. Hughes, a historian of technology who wanted other historians to pay much more attention to the development of the systems that surround our lives. Hughes argued that historians had failed to take account of the 'massive, extensive, vertically integrated production systems of the modern world' (T. P. Hughes, *Networks of Power, Electrification in Western Society, 1880–1930* [Baltimore, MD: Johns Hopkins University Press, 1983], p. 5). By this he meant that the discipline had largely neglected the incredible feats of human endeavour that had transformed our everyday urban life, particularly from the 1800s onwards. Hughes studied the electrification of Western society and explored in rich detail how visible, physical artefacts such as turbo-generators, transformers, electric transmission lines and entire electric light and power systems could only be brought into being by a vast collective effort. Hughes's work demonstrated how the historical contexts of different places profoundly affected the material and social effort needed to electrify California, London, Berlin and Chicago. Large technical systems depend on organizations such as manufacturing firms, utility companies and investment banks; they require natural resources such as coal mines and forests; institutional knowledge such as books, articles and university teaching programmes; and legislative artefacts such as laws and standards. Hughes was able to show that the development of the

electricity system in Berlin was deeply influenced by a productive working relationship between industry, technology and local politics, while in contrast very similar material technologies were deployed much more slowly, and in very different ways, in London due to a long-standing ideological divide between municipal provision and private enterprise, which manifested in political-legislative delays and fragmentation. This left London, in the early 1900s, as the largest and richest city in the Western world, but simultaneously the poorest in terms of electric power provision.

4 For instance, many Orthodox Jews in New York City bought expensive water filters after discovering that they could be ingesting an amoeba which, though harmless to health, is considered unkosher. J. Berger, 'Water's fine but is it kosher?', *New York Times*, 7 November 2004, https://www.nytimes.com/2004/11/07/nyregion/the-waters-fine-but-is-it-kosher.html (accessed 17 October 2019).

5 N. Anand, 'Pressure: the politechnics of water supply in Mumbai', *Cultural Anthropology* 26.4 (2011), pp. 542–64.

6 D. H. Meadows, *Thinking in Systems: A Primer* (White River Junction, VT: Chelsea Green Publishing, 2008).

7 F. W. Geels, 'The hygienic transition from cesspools to sewer systems (1840–1930): the dynamics of regime transformation', *Research Policy* 35.7 (2006), pp. 1069–82.

8 T. J. Foxon, 'A coevolutionary framework for analysing a transition to a sustainable low carbon economy', *Ecological Economics* 70.12 (2011), pp. 2258–67.

9 B. Fine and E. Leopold, *The World of Consumption* (London: Routledge, 1993).

10 See also C. Arnsperger and Y. Varoufakis, 'What is neoclassical economics? The three axioms responsible for its theoretical oeuvre, practical irrelevance and, thus, discursive power', *Panoeconomicus* 53.1 (2006), pp. 5–18, DOI: http://dx.doi.org/10.2298/PAN0601005A.

11 Fine also critiques a structuralism used by the other side of the debate, which frames the market for a commodity as a construct of, *inter alia*, monopolistic capital, manipulative advertising and consumer ignorance. Fine charts a middle ground by proposing that commodities are shaped by the degrees of competition and rationality in markets and the sociocultural meanings attached to

specific commodities. B. Fine, *The World of Consumption: The Material and Cultural Revisited* (Abingdon: Routledge, 2002).

12 For systems of provision examples, see K. Bayliss, B. Fine and M. Robertson, 'From financialisation to consumption: the systems of provision approach applied to housing and water', FESSUD Working Paper 02 (2013), http://eprints.soas.ac.uk/16844/1/FESSUD-Working-Paper-02-.pdf (accessed 17 October 2019).

13 Fine, Bayliss and Robertson, 'The systems of provision approach to understanding consumer culture', p. 30.

14 One regional provider, Yorkshire Water, is a private company owned by Kelda Group, which is in turn owned by Saltaire Water, which is owned by Citibank and HSBC holdings. The English experience of water privatization was particularly aggressive, since the Thatcher administration actually *sold* rather than leased the entirety of the sector into private hands. Subsequently many water companies have been taken off the stock exchange by larger institutional investors. These companies, including Yorkshire Water, have been subjected to a series of accounting practices, debt swaps, tax offshoring and financial engineering that has left many English consumers paying almost one-third of their water bills to satisfy interest and dividend payments of parent companies. K. Bayliss, 'Material cultures of water financialisation in England and Wales', *New Political Economy* 22.4 (2017), pp. 383–97, DOI: 10.1080/13563467.2017.1259300.

15 Horizontal approaches apply common theories across different commodities. Economists use utility maximization, postmodernists use semiotics, sociologists use emulation and distinction, and so on. The specific commodity is only the starting point for the application of a theory, not the object of interest on its own. It is not that horizontal ideas such as gender norms, construction and identity are not a factor in how one consumes cars, for example, but they can obscure the material reality of how the cars came to be, how the road was built to carry them, how the fuel was extracted to run them, if they are applied without similar critical attention to vertical systems. K. Raworth, *Doughnut Economics: Seven Ways to Think like a 21st-century Economist* (White River Junction, VT: Chelsea Green Publishing, 2017); E. A. Van den Hende and R. Mugge,

'Investigating gender-schema congruity effects on consumers' evaluation of anthropomorphized products', *Psychology & Marketing* 31.4 (2014), pp. 264–77.

16 C. Liddell, C. Morris, H. Thomson and C. Guiney, 'Excess winter deaths in 30 European countries 1980–2013: a critical review of methods', *Journal of Public Health* 38.4 (2016), pp. 806–14.

17 R. Larsson, 'A comparative case study of non-technical barriers for combined heat and power and district heating diffusion in Sweden and the United Kingdom', MSc thesis, Cranfield University at Silsoe, 2006, https://stud.epsilon.slu.se/10862/1/larsson_r_170925.pdf (accessed 17 October 2019).

18 L. Carroli and M. Guaralda, 'Cycling in Indian cities: a changing cultural narrative of citizenship, urbanism and cycling', in *Sustainable Cities in Asia* (London: Routlege, 2017), pp. 203–12.

19 M. Anantharaman, 'Elite and ethical: the defensive distinctions of middle-class bicycling in Bangalore, India', *Journal of Consumer Culture* 17.3 (2017), pp. 864–86.

20 A. T. Ghate, *Pedalling Towards a Greener India: A Report on Promoting Cycling in the Country* (New Delhi: TERI, 2014), http://www.teriin.org/eventdocs/files/Cycling_Report_LR.pdf (accessed 17 October 2019).

21 M. Verma, T. M. Rahul, P. V. Reddy and A. Verma, 'The factors influencing bicycling in the Bangalore city', *Transportation Research Part A: Policy and Practice* 89 (2016), pp. 29–40.

22 W. Steffen et al., 'Planetary boundaries: guiding human development on a changing planet', *Science* 347.6223 (2015), pp. 1–10.

23 D. W. O'Neill, A. L. Fanning, W. F. Lamb and J. K. Steinberger, 'A good life for all within planetary boundaries', *Nature Sustainability* 1 (2018), pp. 88–95, DOI: 10.1038/s41893–018–0021–4; Raworth, *Doughnut Economics*.

24 E. B. Barbier, *A Global Green New Deal: Rethinking the Economic Recovery* (Cambridge: Cambridge University Press, 2010).

25 Many more could be adapted as well. As noted, this is an initial framework, not a complete one.

26 Obvious exceptions are recent anti-carbohydrate diets such as paleo, or observant Jews during Passover.

27 This applies within specific engineering tolerances.

28 J. Millward-Hopkins et al., 'Fully integrated modelling for sustainability assessment of resource recovery from waste', *Science of the Total Environment* 612 (2018), pp. 613–24, DOI: 10.1016/j.scitotenv.2017.08.211.

29 Nobel Laureate Paul Samuelson, a key founder of modern neoclassical economics, is generally credited with this initial division. P. A. Samuelson, 'The pure theory of public expenditure', *The Review of Economics and Statistics* 36.4 (1954), pp. 387–9.

30 R. H. Coase, 'The lighthouse in economics', *The Journal of Law and Economics* 17.2 (1974), pp. 357–76; W. Barnett and W. Block, 'Coase and Van Zandt on lighthouses', *Public Finance Review* 35.6 (2007), pp. 710–33.

31 The term comes from one of the most important theorists of public choice economics, James Buchanan, who won the Nobel Prize in 1986. His political work is now considered the bedrock of the far right economic ideology in the US. J. M. Buchanan, 'An economic theory of clubs', *Economica* 32.125 (1965), pp. 1–14. See L. Parramore, 'Meet the economist behind the one percent's stealth takeover of America', Institure for New Economic Thinking, 30 May 2018, https://www.ineteconomics.org/perspectives/blog/meet-the-economist-behind-the-one-percents-stealth-takeover-of-america (accessed 17 October 2019).

32 V. Ostrom and E. Ostrom, 'A theory for institutional analysis of common pool problems', in G. Hardin and J. Baden (eds), *Managing the Commons* (San Francisco: W.H. Freeman, 1977), pp. 157–72.

33 Ostrom won the Nobel Prize in 2009. See also E. Ostrom, 'Polycentric systems for coping with collective action and global environmental change', *Global Environmental Change* 20.4 (2010), pp. 550–7.

34 G. Hardin, 'The tragedy of the commons', *Science* 162 (1968), pp. 1243–8.

35 L. A. Fennell, 'Ostrom's Law: property rights in the commons', *International Journal of the Commons* 5.1 (2011), pp. 9–27 (p. 9).

36 Ibid., p. 18.

37 This only becomes more true if we move beyond resource-intensive

reliance systems to ones based more in human capital, for example healthcare, education, media, policing, etc.

38 See also A. Bowman, I. Ertürk, J. Froud, S. Johal and J. Law, *The End of the Experiment? From Competition to the Foundational Economy* (Manchester: Manchester University Press, 2014), and J. Earle, C. Moran and Z. Ward-Perkins, *The Econocracy* (Manchester: Manchester University Press, 2016).

39 See A. Schafran, *The Road to Resegregation: Northern California and the Failure of Politics* (Berkeley, CA: University of California Press, 2018) for a review of regionalism as an ideology in urban planning.

40 For instance, a second way of defining 'collective consumption', generally associated with Castells, defines it primarily through the role of the state in propping up or providing the means of consumption. According to this view, these objects are necessary for the reproduction of labour power, and hence the reproduction of capitalism, but as they had (at the time) limited possibilities for profit, the state intervenes. As Cox and Jonas put it pithily, this school of collective consumption thought has 'the socialization of consumption by the state' as 'a common denominator' (K. R. Cox and A. E. Jonas, 'Urban development, collective consumption and the politics of metropolitan fragmentation', *Political Geography* 12.1 [1993], pp. 8–37 [p. 11]). The state-centred version of collective consumption is more common than Lojkine's understanding, in part because it became central to Castells's understanding of urban social movements – the fight for collective consumption, defined in this way through the role of the state, was the first of three reasons why he argued that urban social movements come together. This is also why collective consumption is now popular again – people are increasingly fighting for these collectively produced goods, in a way that shows the state-centred definition to be problematic. Social movements are not necessarily demanding state provision, simply an intervention, now that foundational urban systems 'can be productively plundered, used to actively generate capital, used (and abused) in evermore exploitative and extractive rounds of primitive accumulation' (A. Merrifield, Intervention – 'Crammed contested strip: democracy in the New Republic', *Antipode* blog, 25 June 2014, https://antipode online.org/2014/06/25/crammed-contested-strip/, accessed 13

January 2020). See Castells and Sheridan, 'The urban question: a Marxish approach'; Castells, *The City and the Grassroots*; Lojkine, 'Marxist theory of capitalist urbanization'.

41 T. Crewe, 'The strange death of municipal England', *London Review of Books* 38.24 (15 December 2016), pp. 6–10; E. Swyngedouw, 'Dispossessing H2O: the contested terrain of water privatization', *Capitalism Nature Socialism* 16.1 (2005), pp. 81–98.

42 For example, see how Ecotricity enters and participates in the UK energy market, https://www.ecotricity.co.uk/?gclid=EAIaIQ obChMI5vPf9O7d3QIVSLTtCh1rEg_tEAAYASAAEgKEPvD_ BwE (accessed 17 October 2019).

43 E. Charmes, 'Carte scolaire et «clubbisation» des petites communes périurbaines', *Sociétés contemporaines* 3 (2007), pp. 67–94.

44 E. McKenzie, *Privatopia: Homeowner Associations and the Rise of Residential Private Government* (New Haven, CT: Yale University Press, 1994); F. Chiodelli and V. Baglione, 'Living together privately: for a cautious reading of cohousing', *Urban Research & Practice* 7.1 (2014), pp. 20–34.

45 See, for instance, the debate on the differences between gated communities and co-housing. M. L. Ruiu, 'Differences between cohousing and gated communities. A literature review', *Sociological Inquiry* 84.2 (2014), pp. 316–35; F. Chiodelli, 'Differences and similarities among cohousing, gated communities and other kinds of homeowners associations: a reply to Ruiu', *GSSI Urban Studies Working Paper* 22 (2015), https://papers.ssrn.com/sol3/papers.cfm?abstract_id=2597485 (accessed 17 October 2019).

46 N. Srnicek and A. Williams, *Inventing the Future: Postcapitalism and a World without Work* (London: Verso, 2015).

47 M. Bookchin, 'Libertarian municipalism: an overview', *Green Perspectives* 24 (1991), pp. 1–6.

48 B. Born and M. Purcell, 'Avoiding the local trap scale and food systems in planning research', *Journal of Planning Education and Research* 26.2 (2006), pp. 195–207 (pp. 195–6).

49 A. Gouldson et al., 'Innovative financing models for low carbon transitions: exploring the case for revolving funds for domestic energy efficiency programmes', *Energy Policy* 86 (2015), pp. 739–48, DOI: 10.1016/j.enpol.2015.08.012.

50 Retrofitting in this way can be considered a type of 'non-reform-
    ist reform' *à la* Gorz and Fraser. See N. Fraser and A. Honneth,
    *Redistribution   or   Recognition?   A   Political-Philosophical
    Exchange* (London: Verso, 2003).
51 We are working on developing a broader version for public
    use based on this model. This is a necessarily simplified version
    given the space and readability requirements of this book.

3   Seeing like a settlement

In the previous chapter, we outlined an initial analytical framework for examining systems from the ground up. Any reformed spatial contracts must be based on the specific ways in which systems differ from each other. Applied to the disposal of human waste, a system-centred perspective would seek to understand the historical development of any given system. It would examine cultural feelings towards waste and the power dynamics in a given area with regard to who gets sewerage. It would understand the provision and education of sanitary engineers, the building of treatment plants and the rules and regulations associated with sewerage. The notion of substitutability would help us think about whether composting toilets could provide a better alternative in some situations, the notion of rivalry and excludability would help us analyse how overburdened the system is, or the problems associated with excluding people from the system.

The goal of the last chapter was to help develop a systems-centred perspective that is detached from ideology, whether it was ideology attached to sectors or institutional types, or ideology attached to geographical scale. Rather than toss out the categories used by ideologues of different stripes, we argued instead that they can be turned into an analytical framework for better understanding the differences between reliance systems. This is a critical step in building a healthier spatial contract.

Yet there is a limit to any approach that simply seeks to

pull things apart. A system is always more than the sum of its parts. Obviously, systems interact with each other. Waste disposal and sanitary systems are vital to any number of other reliance systems, and vice versa. Reliance systems also always exist somewhere, even if that place is virtual. An effective analytical framework for reliance systems must be able to understand how, in the words of the late geographer Edward Soja, 'it all comes together' in space and place, or more precisely, in human settlements.[1]

In virtually every society on earth, there are ideologies that primarily adhere to reliance systems when they come together in space and place. These ideologies can be as deeply ingrained in political culture as ideologies of scale and sector and institution. Seemingly interconnected places may have distinct ways of life, distinct senses of who they are and what they do, distinct visions of how to provision reliance systems. There may also be long-standing inequalities in how and where and to whom and at what cost reliance systems are provisioned across space and place, inequalities that make any coming together politically extremely difficult. In order to truly understand how these cultural ideologies become political barriers to a healthier spatial contract, we must see how they come together in settlements.

The first step in this process is to avoid simply seeing reliance systems as artefacts that exist in cities and towns, or merely as the by-product of urbanization or industrialization. Inspired by a growing movement in urban studies to see the city as an assemblage of systems, we must see reliance systems as part of the very essence of human settlements.[2] By this we mean *all* settlements, regardless of shape, size, location, legality or temporality. Both the refugee camp and the great metropolis are settlements, and both are assemblages of systems.

In many ways, *these systems are our settlements*, and our settlements are a collection of systems. Reliance systems enable us to live collectively, and we live collectively in part to enable the collective provision of these systems. This inextricable link between systems and settlements is part of why we insist on calling our revision and revitalization of the social contract 'the spatial contract'. The 'spatial' forces us to appreciate the way in which these systems are inextricably and historically embedded in geography more generally, and in human settlements more specifically.

The goal of this chapter is thus to develop the corollary to 'seeing like a system' – seeing like a settlement, a way of seeing systems as they come together in space and place that illuminates ideological divides. Critical to this perspective is an at times painful (and linguistically specific) attention to language. We begin by explaining why we don't use the terms urban or municipal services, connecting this chapter to the previous chapter's work on ideology. We then explain why we talk throughout this book in terms of settlements, instead of talking of cities or 'the urban' or urbanization, focusing on how the many ways in which we name our settlements have helped perpetuate two key spatial and institutional divides. These divides are intricately related to the provision of reliance systems, and can either be exposed or reproduced depending on how we define and discuss the settlements–systems linkage.

The first set of ideological divides are the various spatial divisions that exist in some form but in different ways virtually everywhere: the divides between urban and rural, between city and town or village, between city and suburb, etc. The second are also virtually everywhere, even if many in the Global North would like to pretend it is a Southern phenomenon: the divides between informal and formal, and the related but different divide between legal and illegal.

While scholars and activists have worked diligently over the years in an attempt to show that both sets of divisions are often unwarranted, unhelpful and unscientific, they remain politically and culturally very real in different ways in different places. Like the sectoral, institutional and scalar fixations discussed in the previous chapters, most people in most places will have to confront an entrenched politics of provision that follows the contours of one or both forms of division. Seeing systems through human settlements makes these divisions clearer, so that we can build a healthier spatial contract along more productive lines.

Human settlements as an operating framework

One of the most common ways to think about reliance systems is through the lens of urban or municipal services. Roads, 'public' transport, sewers, water systems, police and fire officers, rubbish collection, even education and healthcare are often described by policymakers, academics, engineers and the general public as services in this way.

We do not use the term services for a number of reasons. First and foremost, it reinforces the passive relationship that too many of us have to the basic systems that allow us to act. If creating a positive feedback loop between action and the systems that enable us to act is an integral part of a healthier spatial contract, calling them services doesn't help. Thinking in terms of services can make us forget the vast and diverse agency that went into these systems in the first place, often masking what it really takes to make the tap produce water, or to render the streets safe.

Second, the urban or municipal services framework also reinforces false assumptions regarding who is and who should be part of providing these systems. Both of the main ideologies discussed in the previous chapter – our imagination of the ideal sector or scale for collective provisioning of these systems – are perpetuated when we call them urban or municipal services. While local government – which is what most mean by the urban or municipal in this context – surely plays a vital role in collective provisioning, naming it in this way obscures the full system of provision, even in places with strong and well-resourced local governments.

Third, the concept of urban services can also reinforce rural imaginations – and imaginations of the rural – as places where reliance systems are absent. While certain systems are absent in many rural places – broadband internet, sewerage, or simply electricity – these communities do have systems for communication, waste disposal and energy provision. In some of the poorest urban parts of the world, reliance systems for communication, waste and energy may not be dramatically different from what they were in the village.

Fourth, by naming some systems after the institution that we imagine provisions them, or the geography in which we imagine they exist, the services framework ignores important reliance systems that have historically had less state involvement. Why is healthcare not a municipal service or an urban service (in some places it is)? What about finance (in many places it is)? Take, for instance, food. Rarely if ever will you find food talked about as a municipal service, even if the state may be heavily involved in food safety and in ensuring basic access to adequate food through direct distribution or cash transfers, even if local governments may help support or sustain local markets or provide direct meals through schools and social service agencies. Simply because certain institutions at a certain time and place played a key role in provisioning these systems does not mean that we can define them as such.[3]

Avoiding the 'services' trap is vital *because* virtually all reliance systems are fundamentally embedded materially *and* socially in the places that humans have built and occupy, and these places and the systems that form them are incredibly diverse. Reliance systems are central to the formation of all shapes and sizes and forms of settlement. A large metropolis may have a greater number and complexity and variety of reliance systems, but even the smallest of encampments and hamlets can be seen as a collection of systems.

This is true of both permanent and temporary settlements. A camp may be a temporary settlement – or it may be imagined to be when it is built – but what defines it in many ways is that it is constructed so as to provide certain core systems, both materially (tents, cooking equipment, etc.), geographically (location vis-à-vis water, wind) and socially (who does what within the camp). Migrants, nomadic peoples, travellers, campers, retirees in motorhomes and any number of other types of mobile people still *rely* on systems for action. These systems may or may not be safe, secure, well-functioning, reliable or resilient, but just because a place is temporary does not mean they don't exist, and it doesn't mean we should view reliance systems as somehow detached from settlement.

The camp is also an excellent illustration of how reliance systems must be seen as intrinsically linked to settlements. Even when a settlement is only temporary, or forced upon people in the most desperate of circumstances, systems are developed internally to the settlement in order to realize human agency. A refugee camp and a motorhome park structure agency in different ways for very different reasons, but the core relationship between systems and settlements remains.

Why a 'seeing like a settlement' perspective is necessary

Seeing like a settlement avoids fixation on particular systems, losing sight of the wood for the trees. While there is no denying that certain forms of expertise and labour must focus on waste disposal, a new politics of waste disposal must incorporate a broader view.[4] This includes water to feed the system; cultural relations to waste and working with waste; the specific densities of human settlement; soil types, drainage, slope and other physical geographical functions; the often complex and overlapping governance structures that can include everyone from the local state and international NGOs to multinational corporations; and small-scale entrepreneurs or labourers. Seeing this particular reliance system through the settlements in which it occurs maintains this wider focus.

At the same time, it helps us from getting lost in 'systems of systems' and in 'complexity', in the often vague language of infrastructures or metabolism. While it may be true that 'it's all related and connected, man', this fact does not help us understand how. If we want to understand how systems intersect and interact, what better place to start than with where they interact? Agency, or human freedom, is highly specific, and must be constantly reproduced in actual spaces and places. The more we learn about the evolution and development of human settlements, the more we realize that specificities matter as much as generalities, especially in rapidly changing parts of the world.[5]

The settlement perspective is also vital in understanding the accumulation of previous existing systems, beyond the systems framework delineated in the previous chapter. A new politics of provisioning, a new and healthier spatial contract, cannot be built around the idea that we can or should throw everything out and start over. No matter how much we may love and embrace new technology, new ways of provisioning and new systems will always only ever be a retrofit – an injection of new ideas and new ways of doing things into much older systems. This is true for both very fixed systems such as housing and more mobile systems such as policing. This is true in places with well-functioning systems, and in those where it appears from the outside that nothing works. Seeing our settlements as an accumulation of systems – some of which are obsolete or barely used or falling apart – reminds us that a new spatial contract is not a utopia written on a blank slate, but rather a set of actions that take place in a history that is all around us.

One of the reasons why it is difficult to see systems through settlements is the English language. The basic English-language vocabulary of human settlements – city, village, metropolis, urban, rural, suburban, etc. – is notoriously varied in its meaning, both within and between cultures. Is a city a political creature, defined by lines on a map or by a particular ruler or government? Is it a settlement of a certain size or density or heterogeneity, as Louis Wirth famously defined it?[6] Is it an agglomeration defined by economics and commuting patterns? What is the difference between a city and a town, or a village, or a suburb?

The situation becomes even more varied (and contentious) when discussing the processes driving change in settlements – urbanization, suburbanization and so on. As Hillary Angelo and David Wachsmuth ask: 'Which is it: urbanization or the city? One is a process, the other a site that is one (but not the only) outcome of that process. Surely they are not the same thing.'[7] As varying forms of urbanization become a greater and greater force in changing people's lives and changing the planet, our collective vocabulary for settlements and the processes that create and transform them only grows more complex and variegated.

This confusion is understandable, given the long and diverse history of humans living collectively in places. We use the term settlement exclusively in this book so as to be inclusive, for a renewed spatial contract must be built from the needs and wants of all settlements, not from any one person's or group's idealized form of collective living. But the term is also chosen because its awkwardness and blandness illuminate two important sets of political divides in the provision of reliance systems that attach to settlements, divides that hinder political reasoning and collective provision: the divide between urban and rural and everywhere in between, and the divide between the formal and informal. The very idea of using the term settlements, in fact, is taken from an innovative educational project that recognized that making peace between urban and rural was central to the transformation of the systems that sustain us all.

The space and place divides

Over the past decade, scholars and practitioners from different parts of India have been slowly building one of the most ambitious higher education projects – and the most ambitious new reliance systems – on the planet. The ultimate goal is a multi-sited institute, networked throughout India, which will change the way India teaches and learns and builds and governs core reliance systems. When the first campus in Bengaluru is complete, it will include up to ten new schools, focused on everything from systems and infrastructure to human and economic development, with innovative educational programmes designed to reach both formal and informal practitioners in cities and villages throughout India.[8]

Like many projects of its kind, it is specifically being constructed with the knowledge that urbanization is a central driving force in people's lives across the world, and nowhere more so than India. The institute recognizes the need to see systems through the lens of urbanization, through spaces and places. As it states clearly in its mission statement, the institute sees 'urbanisation as the core of a new knowledge paradigm that provides the scaffolding for a new, interdisciplinary, 21st century University'.[9]

But this new institute is not called the Indian Institute for Urbanization, or the Indian Institute for Cities. Instead, it has the decidedly more awkward name of the Indian Institute for Human Settlements (IIHS). It is a name that no marketing executive or branding consultant would have come up with. If the goal had been to create a shiny new facility to sell to foreigners, they would have chosen something sexier.[10]

But settlements as a naming device represented a critical *political* compromise – a recognition that in the spatial politics of India, any naming that even hinted at favouritism towards either the city or the village was a political non-starter.[11] The founders of IIHS recognized that they are not simply building new technical knowledges about systems, but political ones as well. While many involved in the project probably define urbanization as a process that includes everywhere from the smallest village to the largest central city, the imagined dichotomy between urban and rural, between cities and villages, remains culturally and politically salient. Gandhi's famous phrase that 'India lives in her villages and not in her towns' was specifically aimed at the educated class in urban areas.[12] The fact that millions of people have migrated from villages to large cities, and that large urban areas have sprawled into the countryside – turning villages into suburbs and even small cities – has not consigned this divide to the dustbin of history.

The same is true in radically different contexts throughout the world. In France, farmers burning tyres in protest about agricultural policy and the challenges of rural life in the contemporary economy remain culturally very distant from young people burning cars in the stigmatized corners of the *banlieue*, even if they are literally right next door to each other in many regions. In colonial Africa, British administrators purposely rolled out different forms of colonial rule in urban and rural areas in order to prevent collective action.[13] In the United Kingdom, anti-urban sentiment born in part from a romanticized love of village life hasn't necessarily ebbed, even though most rural villages are functionally suburbs on one of the most urbanized islands on the planet. In the United States, fully 84 per cent of the population of the country was classified by the 2010 census as living in a 'metropolitan area'.[14] This means that the county you live in has strong enough social economic connections to a central county which meets certain complex criteria for being 'urban'.[15] But it means little from a cultural perspective, from a political perspective, and lines between imagined rural, suburban and urban places still affect everything from cultural politics to transport funding.[16]

For almost two generations, scholars of urbanization have been pointing out that the basic language we use in English to describe the different sizes and types of places in which we live is unscientific. There is no universally accepted way to *scientifically* define city or suburb, urban or rural, town or village, metropolitan or non-metropolitan.[17] As Neil Brenner and Christian Schmid have demonstrated, the famed statement that 'half the world lives in cities' is a half-truth at best, one based on suspect methodologies and arbitrary definitions.[18] The number is probably far higher, even if one does not understand settlements through reliance systems (as we do) or does not adopt an understanding of 'planetary urbanization' based on resource linkages to growing conurbations, as do Brenner and Schmid.

But no matter how much urban studies scholars attempt to debunk cultural understandings of spatial divisions, rename them in postmodern ways, or try to get us to focus on processes instead of places, the deep-seated cultural meaning of these divides remains. Whether examined through voting patterns or identity, these seemingly arbitrary divisions still matter to people, no matter whether the world around them has changed. Just because your village is now a suburb, your suburb is now a village, your rural community is now exurban or a tourist destination, etc., this does not *necessarily* mean that your sense of place has wavered.

Urban, rural, suburb, city, town, village

Rural studies scholars have also long recognized that, despite being an 'artificial construction', the urban/rural divide is one of the 'oldest and most resilient geographical dualisms'.[19] Even if, as rural geographer Michael Woods has pointed out, 'drawing a boundary line between urban and rural space on a map' is a difficult task,[20] Raymond Williams's famous observation about the divide between the 'country' and the 'city' lives on. This 'artificial construction' continues to have economic, cultural and political meaning, and economic, cultural and political power.

Part of the reason for this is that states have etched these divisions into the landscape. As planner and urban theorist Ananya Roy has worked to make clear, when a government declares one place urban and one place rural, this matters to resource allocation, political power, representation, levels of investment and more.[21] In the language of the spatial contract, while urban and rural residents may actually utilize very similar reliance systems, the spatial contract is very different depending on the legal-political lines. The fact that these terms have different legal and political meaning in different countries – in addition to cultural ones – only adds to the confusion.

For the purpose of the spatial contract, what is vital is to be able to appreciate that these cultural differences are real, regardless of the constructed, artificial or performative nature of these divides.[22] We cannot simply wish them away. As Barbara Ching and Gerald Creed argue in an edited volume which brings together studies of rural culture from contexts as different as Trinidad, Israel and the United States, 'no amount of "development" can obliterate the continuing economic importance or cultural distinctiveness of the countryside'.[23] But what we can resist is what comes next in Ching and Creed's otherwise prescient statement. Their full statement is

> no amount of 'development' can obliterate the continuing economic importance or cultural distinctiveness of the countryside, *where food is produced and human life sustained.* (emphasis added)

If we recognize these geographical boundaries as cultural and politically real yet fundamentally constructed, we must be careful not to reinforce false differences. When it comes to the production of reliance systems, 'human life' is sustained through a complex set of interactions that include virtually every type of space. Scholars and writers from urban, suburban and rural life can all be guilty of what can be considered an ecology of the proper place – that is, a mix of romanticization and denigration that elevates certain types of places as synonymous with a good or just or sustainable life. We must accept that human life is sustained – and can be sustained well – at virtually every gradient density and every type of place.

We must also be careful not to overplay the role that certain types of spaces play in the production of human agency in an interconnected world. Even food production, which may appear to happen in low-density open spaces, actually involves vast systems of knowledge and technological production, transportation networks, governance and market structures, cultural imaginations and so on. Some of these involve large cities, others involve very small cities, which may sit nestled in the countryside and be rural culturally yet still functionally cities, with centralized grids, denser human habitations and so on.

Moreover, fixed conceptions of agency-spatial relations make it difficult to understand, cope with or drive change. Suburban areas can also have a strong sense of cultural identity. Just like rural areas, these are often imagined and performed. Just like rural areas, these are rapidly changing economically and socially, as a 'post-suburban' reality of growing suburban job centres becomes a reality throughout the world.[24] So even if suburban imaginations do not change, the fundamental reliance systems are changing – whether anyone likes it or not.

The statement that we cannot assume any particular spatial relationship to reliance systems is not a normative one, but simply a fact – much as we argued against any assumed sectoral or institutional relationship to the quality of provision of agency in the previous chapter. While we can respect identities and imaginaries as real, a healthy spatial contract will require that we work to bridge these divides. A healthy food system will require collaboration and cooperation across these cultural divides, and this must start by remembering that virtually all humans, regardless of the density or geography of their settlements, derive basic action from reliance systems.

'Rural' residents may be more likely to use non-networked systems for enabling a disease-free life, more urban and suburban residents may use networked systems, but we all use collectively provisioned systems. 'Rural' residents may be more involved in the act of growing food, but the food system has long involved complex markets in larger settlements, knowledge bases produced in university towns and large cities, technological development heavily reliant on manufactured goods brought in from a large network and so on. Even if one discounts 'urban' agriculture as a minor millennial trend – we do not – or even if we ignore the vast peri-urban spaces in which economies are deeply interconnected both to agricultural and extractive industries and major metropolitan centres, 'rural' areas are only one very important node in a larger reliance system for the production of food.

Overcoming space and place divides

In an influential 2007 article, Pablo Gutman, an environmental economist for the World Wildlife Fund, called for a new 'rural–urban compact'.[25] By this he means a revision of the basic deal in which rural communities send people and (generally raw) goods to urban areas in exchange for (generally finished) goods, services and governance. He argues that this informal compact has existed for a thousand years, and needs to be revised. Rural areas are growing more and more impoverished and abandoned, he states, and the environmental damage caused by this system is mounting. His idea for a 'new' compact involves what ecological economists call 'payment for ecosystems services', that is, convincing urban residents to pay for environmental preservation.

Michael Woods critiques Gutman's vision of a new deal for rural residents in large part because 'it conceives of the rural in purely economic and environmental terms. No consideration is given to the social or cultural dimensions of the rural, in particular to the question of whether rural communities would accept this change in function.'[26] From a settlements perspective, Gutman's vision of the original compact is also fraught with historical inaccuracies, oversights and gross generalizations. It too reinforces misconceptions about the connection between agency and space. But the idea of a new compact, of a new political/economic deal between different types of places, is important. This is the type of language we need to be using, and if Gutman's phrasing is reinterpreted and his ideas given more nuance and historical depth, it is something that can be built upon politically.

Hence the dire need to upscale IIHS's political compromise, so as to transform the spirit of Gutman's compact into a healthier spatial contract. First, we must accept that all settlements, regardless of size or type of economic base or cultural identity, rely on collectively provisioned systems. Second, it is political reality in most nations that cooperation between settlements of different types is vital for any meaningful changes in the spatial contract. New transportation-based reliance systems cannot be built without the political cooperation of residents across the spatial spectrum. The same applies to food, water, energy and many more. A new spatial contract is only possible if we find a way to walk the line between recognizing cultural differences across spatial divisions and not reinforcing them.

The goal from a spatial contract perspective must be to make political peace across settlement types. This would be simpler if it were the only major division highlighted by seeing systems through settlements. There is, however, another division, which although not as embedded culturally as the space and place divides, is more embedded legally and politically, for it gets to the root of the question of what is legal: the question of informality.

The legal divides: formality, informality, legality, illegality

From the perspective of a healthier spatial contract, the naming of the Indian Institute for Human Settlements was a critical act, as it recognized and tried not to reproduce divides that directly impacted its ability to enact change in the development of other reliance systems throughout India. Yet the necessity of IIHS as a reliance system goes far beyond this act of naming, and beyond the need for more education or more educated professionals. IIHS was created to educate differently, to be a *different type of reliance system that could produce different modalities of freedom*. It is being designed from the ground up to understand and meet the specific needs of a massive and massively diverse country in the Global South. As a growing chorus of scholars from different parts of the world have argued, integral to a bespoke 'southern approach' is one that integrates informal (and often illegal) ways of producing agency into our basic understanding of how things are done.[27]

This institutional engagement with the division between informality and formality and legality and illegality is vital, as fundamentally this political barrier is institutional as much as or more than cultural. While the space and place divides inhere in institutions and in formal politics, the cultural power of these divisions is what sustains them, even as experts bemoan them. The formal/informal divides, on the other hand, have been built and sustained by experts and the law, often *against* cultural practices. Challenging how we see the legality of reliance systems is a vital first action in this arena. Fortunately, this work is well underway.

Seeing informality

Similar to our discussion about avoiding a normative fixation on any sector, scale or settlement type – that is, assuming that a reliance system is automatically better because of one of these factors – scholars and policymakers and activists associated with this 'southern approach' neither demonize nor fetishize informality, as have been the two most common approaches to date. They simply treat informality, illegality and many other supposed deviations from an imagined norm as part of the landscape that must be dealt with. They examine and understand systems and places as they are, not as they wish them to be.

The demonization of informal systems by technicians, scholars and politicians alike emerged in part because they appear contrary to the large, centralized systems which came to dominate Western regions during the modernist era. From the earliest nineteenth-century sewerage and water systems to later systems of centralized electricity generation, education and healthcare, many began to associate successful reliance systems with generally large-scale, heavily formalized and often bureaucratic systems. To be modern meant to have formal, legible and legal systems, part of what geographers Stephen Graham and Simon Marvin would call the 'integrated ideal'.[28]

As the largest of the settlements throughout the southern hemisphere exploded in the latter part of the twentieth century, and reliance systems repeatedly failed to keep up with need and demand, the simplistic answer to the problem was to point to informality and illegality as the problem. But scholars and activists began to point out the many problems with this approach.

First and foremost, the demonization of informality was often used by those in power as an excuse to bulldoze and evict, often in the name of providing 'better' systems.[29] While 'better' may have meant better for some, it meant the utter destruction of agential capacities for many, especially those deemed illegal or unworthy in some way. New systems were often less affordable, creating tension between the consumption of equally vital systems, where under the informal system multiple complementary systems were affordable, if unreliable or unstable. The development of new systems often meant people being pushed out of place and relocated. While in some cases former residents were provided with a house in a faraway location, this relocation destroyed other reliance systems that residents of informal communities require highly specific social bonds in order to access – for example, the neighbour who can watch your children so that you can work and pay for access to other vital systems.

A second issue was that informality was often seen as a failure, a result of the incapacity of the state. People were left to their own devices by a blind or weak state, or so the theory went. But as Roy and others have worked to demonstrate, informal systems were actually a reliance system of a nefarious kind, a means of producing a particular type of power for certain institutional actors. Allowing land and water and housing and energy to be developed in a seemingly haphazard or informal way was integral to political networks and agglomerations of power. It may not have been by design, but it was not out of ignorance either.[30]

A third problem is that informality was often seen as a temporary step towards formalized, centralized systems for the provision of agency. Informality was thus seen as some sort of pre-modern means of provisioning, one that would ultimately follow the same pathway as in the North and the West. Formal, often centralized reliance systems were imagined as the future pathway.

A fourth issue is that informal and illegal reliance systems are not the exclusive purview of the poor. Roy's work demonstrated that many parts of Calcutta reserved for the wealthiest classes were just as informal or illegal as many prototypical shanties of the poor. While many scholars of informality use informal settlements as a means of avoiding the pejorative terminology of the slum, informality and illegality cannot be seen as synonymous with poverty.

These four points are part of the generalized creation of a set of interlocking ideologies about informality and illegality that permeate many discussions of reliance systems and the poor in the urban Global South. Yet as with sectors, scales and settlement types, different degrees of formality and even legality are appropriate for different systems in different places.

Beyond fixation, fetishization and demonization

As with sectors, scales or institutional form, we don't in any way mean that central or local state provision is not at times a great idea, or that the integrated ideal is not at times actually ideal. Sometimes big and formal is the best way, sometimes not. Just because the urbanist AbdouMaliq Simone would have us recognize 'people as infrastructure', and think about building human agency with this as a fact of life, does not mean that he is advocating the replacement of central sewers with nightsoil collectors, or equating the two.[31] To argue that for most residents in most large cities in most countries life is about what Alex Vaseduvan calls the makeshift (literally make + shift, that is, do something and be prepared to have to move and do it again) is not to argue that it should be this way.[32]

Roy, Simone, Vaseduvan and the many other scholars who we have relied on in this book simply show that many aspects of informal collective provision are deeply ingrained in collective provisioning, and that we discount, demonize or fetishize them at our peril. These progressive and contemporary views of informality have been central to our conceptualization of the spatial contract, as they rigorously and intently work to understand place-specific forms of human freedom, integrating formal and informal and everywhere in between. In a given situation, perhaps the density of human habitation demands that formal, centralized sewerage be retrofitted through a settlement, as that is the only system that will enable the act of disease-free life. But this can come with different permutations of toilet facilities, different degrees of formalized or legalized housing, different means of payment.

Take, for instance, energy generation. Informal systems that relied on burning coal or dung or kerosene often had horrible side-effects. But new technologies for wind and solar distribution can be equally decentralized and even informal – for instance, solar panels that power devices directly and do not connect to the grid are rarely the subject of formal permission. A healthier spatial contract for energy in the Global South may never need to pass through some sort of centralized phase. The moves towards appreciating decentralized electricity generation in many ways renders it more informal.[33] Solar and wind generators disconnected from the grid create new reliance systems and new forms of human agency, and this may be appropriate for some places at some times.

The analytical framework, continued

When we combine the analytical frameworks from 'seeing like a settlement' with those evident from 'seeing like a system', what emerges is a basic roadmap for seeing the various ways in which ideology can impact our analysis of reliance systems and spatial contracts. Table 3 summarizes these points.

Unfortunately, the list of political barriers we have identified thus far – the ideologies of sector or institution, the ideology of scale, the culturally tinged ideologies and political divides between settlement types, and the political, institutional and cultural challenge of informality and illegality – is not complete. The two types of division that the settlement perspective elucidates are often produced and reproduced by

Table 3   Ideologies of reliance systems

Category	Common assumptions
Institution	Assumes a type of institution is automatically better suited to provision reliance systems
Scale	Assumes a particular scale is necessarily superior for provisioning reliance systems
Space and place	Assumes that a given space or place is the sole or primary producer of certain types of human agency; assumes a given space may be inherently 'better' at provisioning freedom
Legal	Assumes that either a formal or informal arrangement is inherently better at provisioning freedom

the *radical inequality* in the provisioning of reliance systems. This inequality stems in part from deeply historical forms of exploitation of the relationship between human freedom and reliance systems, the subject of our next chapter.

Notes

1 E. W. Soja, *Postmodern Geographies: The Reassertion of Space in Critical Social Theory* (London: Verso, 1989).
2 Amin and Thrift, *Seeing like a City*; Simone and Pieterse, *New Urban Worlds*, p. 190.
3 This is even more true as we increasingly realize how a very narrow set of experiences during a narrow historical window (the nineteenth- and twentieth-century North Atlantic) played such an outsized role in determining our vocabulary. See Robinson, 'Global and world cities'.
4 Fredericks, *Garbage Citizenship*.
5 G. Bhan, *In the Public's Interest: Evictions, Citizenship, and Inequality in Contemporary Delhi* (Athens, GA: University of Georgia Press, 2016); Caldeira, 'Peripheral urbanization'.
6 L. Wirth, 'Urbanism as a way of life', *American Journal of Sociology* 44.1 (1938), pp. 1–24.
7 H. Angelo and D. Wachsmuth, 'Urbanizing urban political ecology: a critique of methodological cityism', *International Journal of Urban and Regional Research* 39.1 (2015), pp. 16–27 (p. 20).
8 See their website at iihs.co.in
9 Ibid.
10 We recognize that UN Habitat, the primary UN office dealing with housing and urbanization, is formally named the UN Human Settlements Programme, and that this predates IIHS by decades. We use IIHS as the example because it maintains the use of settlements in the name by which it is known, and because the recent nature of its founding shows how these issues remain salient. The naming issue was not resolved by UN Habitat when it was founded in 1978 following the 1976 Habitat I conference.
11 Gautam Bhan, IIHS, personal correspondence with Alex Schafran, 23 February 2018.

12 *The Hindu*, 19 March 1925, 26:302, in *Gandhi on Villages*, ed. Divya Joshi, p. 31, https://www.mkgandhi.org/ebks/ Gandhionvillages.pdf (accessed 17 October 2019).

13 M. Mamdani, *Citizen and Subject: Contemporary Africa and the Legacy of Late Colonialism* (Princeton, NJ: Princeton University Press, 1996).

14 S. G. Wilson, D. A. Plane, P. J. Mackun, T. R. Fischetti and J. Goworowska (with D. T. Cohen, M. J. Perry and G. W. Hatchard), *Patterns of Metropolitan and Micropolitan Population Change: 2000 to 2010*, US Census Report Number C2010sr-01, September 2012, https://www.census.gov/library/ publications/2012/dec/c2010sr-01.html (accessed 12 November 2019). Furthermore, if smaller Micropolitan Areas are included, the United States is 94 per cent 'urban'.

15 Office of Management & Budget, *2010 Standards for Delineating Metropolitan and Micropolitan Statistical Areas; Notice* (PDF), US Government Publishing Office, National Archives and Records Administration, https://www.federalreg ister.gov/documents/2010/06/28/2010-15605/2010-standards- for-delineating-metropolitan-and-micropolitan-statistical-areas (accessed 2 January 2018).

16 S. Hall and A. E. Jonas, 'Urban fiscal austerity, infrastructure provision and the struggle for regional transit in Motor City', *Cambridge Journal of Regions, Economy and Society* 7.1 (2014), pp. 189–206, DOI: 10.1093/cjres/rst031.

17 M. Fragkias, B. Güneralp, K. C. Seto and J. Goodness, 'A synthesis of global urbanization projections', in T. Elmqvist, M. Fragkias, J. Goodness, B. Güneralp, P. J. Marcotullio, R. I. McDonald, S. Parnell, M. Schewenius, M. Sendstad, K. C. Seto and C. Wilkinson (eds), *Urbanization, Biodiversity and Ecosystem Services: Challenges and Opportunities* (Heidelberg: Springer Netherlands, 2013), pp. 409–35.

18 N. Brenner and C. Schmid, 'The "urban age" in question', *International Journal of Urban and Regional Research* 38.3 (2014), pp. 731–55.

19 M. Woods, *Rural* (Abingdon: Routledge, 2010), p. 264.

20 Ibid., p. 2.

21 A. Roy, 'What is urban about critical urban theory?', *Urban Geography* 37.6 (2016), pp. 810–23.

22 Ibid.

23 B. Ching and G. W. Creed (eds), *Knowing your Place: Rural Identity and Cultural Hierarchy* (London: Psychology Press, 1997).

24 N. A. Phelps and F. Wu (eds), *International Perspectives on Suburbanization* (New York: Palgrave Macmillan, 2011).

25 P. Gutman, 'Ecosystem services: foundations for a new rural–urban compact', *Ecological Economics* 62.3–4 (2007), pp. 383–7.

26 Woods, *Rural*, p. 142.

27 Simone and Pieterse, *New Urban Worlds*; Bhan, *In the Public's Interest*; Caldeira, 'Peripheral urbanization', p. 130. See also G. Bhan, S. Srinivas and V. Watson (eds), *The Routledge Companion to Planning in the Global South* (Abingdon: Routledge, 2017).

28 S. Graham and S. Marvin, *Splintering Urbanism: Networked Infrastructures, Technological Mobilities and the Urban Condition* (Abingdon: Routledge, 2002).

29 Bhan, *In the Public's Interest*.

30 A. Roy, *City Requiem, Calcutta: Gender and the Politics of Poverty* (Minneapolis, MN: University of Minnesota Press, 2003).

31 A. Simone, 'People as infrastructure: intersecting fragments in Johannesburg', *Public Culture* 16.3 (2004), pp. 407–29.

32 A. Vasudevan, 'The makeshift city: towards a global geography of squatting', *Progress in Human Geography* 39.3 (2015), pp. 338–59.

33 A. Hirsch, Y. Parag and J. Guerrero, 'Microgrids: a review of technologies, key drivers, and outstanding issues', *Renewable and Sustainable Energy Reviews* 90 (2018), pp. 402–11.

4   Reliance and exploitation

Over the past two chapters we have worked to develop an analytical framework for analysing reliance systems and spatial contracts. Certain assumptions and ideologies about systems can get in the way of developing healthy agreements, which is why we call for a system-centred politics, as opposed to a politics-centred system. When we start to see systems through settlements and vice versa, we also see more clearly other barriers, divides between space and place, and those between the formal and the informal. This much, at least, is required to realize better political agreements that govern the provisioning of basic reliance systems to realize human agency and freedom.

This chapter is about addressing another fundamental obstacle in the pursuit of healthier spatial contracts. The majority of the world has never enjoyed the benefit of a healthy spatial contract. This is true not just in the large metropoles of the Global South, but in most communities in the Global North. This is true in urban communities, rural communities and suburban communities in different ways in different places. In some places, reliance systems, once prevalent and secure, have been undone by neglect, age, privatization or incompetence. In some communities, early-onset climate change is already undermining reliance systems.

If we accept that a core principle of a healthier spatial contract is that actions taken that are enabled by reliance systems must strengthen or reinforce those (or other) reliance systems (Chapter 1), what do we do about those who have been excluded from reliance systems in the first place? How can we expect people to use whatever agency they have been able to muster in the face of inadequate, precarious or exploitative reliance systems to do more than cobble together a precarious way of living? How do we build or advocate for a healthier spatial contract in the face of rampant inequality, domination, oppression and exploitation in the provision of reliance systems? How can we argue for a healthier spatial contract when existing relations between people and the systems they rely on are constantly being undermined or destroyed? It is one thing to demand that those with ample agency realized by an under-appreciated set of reliance systems do more with that agency. It is another to ask that those with much more limited or precarious or hard-won agency contribute in the same way.

Activists, critics and scholars from around the world have shown clearly that inadequate reliance systems in most of the world are not the product of limited resources. Rather, they are the product of very clear relations of oppression, domination and exploitation. A healthier spatial contract must be rooted in a recognition that human agency (and so human freedom) is unequally distributed and precariously realized for most *because of institutional action*, not because of institutional *inaction*. Accordingly, any vision for a healthier spatial contract must recognize the awful truths of how reliance systems have been provisioned.

In this final substantive chapter, we attempt to develop a specific way of understanding the relationship between reliance systems and oppression. This is the final piece of the analytical framework developed over the last two chapters. In this case, we adapt Iris Marion Young's 'five faces of oppression', rearticulating each form of oppression in the language of reliance systems and the spatial contract.

Reliance systems and oppression

In a landmark 1990 book, the late political theorist Iris
Marion Young sought to unpack various forms of oppression and domination.[1] Young's 'five faces of oppression'
– exploitation, marginalization, powerlessness, cultural imperialism and violence – constitute an account of oppression
as a *structural phenomenon*. According to this view, there
is no need for a clear oppressor for oppression to exist. As
a result of certain systemic features of the social order, some
people suffer certain forms of oppression. These systemic
features operate according to their own logic and without
overall planning or guidance by any person or institution.
The concept of oppression is therefore not fit for assigning
personal blame or guiding resentment at a specific individual.
Rather, it is a concept that helps us to determine where
and how to intervene in order to resolve different forms of
oppression.

Young's work was primarily a response to the dominant
Rawlsian account of distributive justice, and in particular
to the view that a radical redistribution of rights, liberties,
income and wealth, and the social bases of self-respect (i.e.,
Rawls's social primary goods) would be sufficient to resolve
the various injustices of oppression. It is a challenge that any
account based around the production and distribution of
'stuff' must face. We face it by showing how Young's analysis
of the five faces of oppression can easily be reworked in terms
of our model of a spatial contract centred on reliance systems.

In this way, this chapter furthers our analytical and
political framework developed in the first three chapters. Like
those efforts, what we propose is meant as an initial framework, not a complete understanding of every facet of oppression. And like Young, we fully acknowledge that the faces of
oppression are linked and not easily separable, but that does
not mean we cannot pull them apart so as to better understand the contours and the differences in how oppression
operates in relation to reliance. Our aim is diagnostic: this

is how seeing politics in terms of a spatial contract centred on reliance systems can help us to understand the nature of oppression.

Exploitation

The first of Young's faces of oppression is exploitation. She builds this account around the Marxian notion of exploitation, although she does not rely on the labour theory of value or some controversial variant of it. Rather, she generalizes away from Marx's specific account of exploitation and characterizes it as a product of 'a steady process of the transfer of the results of [the] labor of one social group to benefit another'.[2] Labour, Young urges, should be conceptualized broadly to include the forms of labour that feminists have long argued that traditional Marxists ignored, such as emotional care and child rearing. For Young, and for us, the concept of exploitation must include structural disadvantages suffered by women, racialized groups and others that take the form of 'the transfer of energies from one group to another to produce an unequal distribution'.[3]

Exploitation understood through the lens of the spatial contract should be understood in terms of the social reproduction of human agency. The organizing idea is that the reliance systems that constitute a powerful group's agency enable that powerful group to use the agency of other social groups in order to increase the powerful group's capacities. Exploitation of reliance systems therefore involves the weakening of others' agency, often within a context of deception. In short, exploitation occurs when a powerful group 'feeds' on the agential capacities of the less powerful.

A reliance systems approach to exploitation that 'sees like a system' reveals how exploitation extends beyond different forms of labour. The end-user of a commodity can be exploited by its vendor, as when monopolists relentlessly raise prices. For example, if an internet service provider has a monopoly in an area, it can charge exorbitant rates and provide poor service. Agential capacities are being

provisioned – people can surf the web, etc. – but it is a predatory form of provisioning.

Part of our argument against a fixation on a certain scale
or sector is that historical examples of exploitation abound
everywhere. Massive telecom giants may exploit in one
country and offer affordable access in another. Local shops
and local stores may offer good deals and quality access to
key systems, or may exploit the fact that they are the only
game in town. Walmart has a detailed history of exploitation of reliance in many ways, but so did many of the older
community stores that it replaced, who often used credit and
their effective monopoly power to exploit local residence
dependence on them as a multi-purpose reliance system.[4]
Public sector and non-profit sector institutions can and have
been guilty of exploiting our basic need for reliance systems.
Exploitation need not come in terms of the monetary costs
extracted for access, but may come in the exchange of power
or patronage through votes for access to reliance, and especially through systems whereby reliance systems are only
constructed for communities that vote a certain way.

A reliance systems view of exploitation therefore goes
beyond labour. But it goes beyond even incorporating exploitation of the end-user. It can also include exploitation of
the land and its products. Clean clothes enable us to leave
the house in socially acceptable terms, enabling us to work,
study or socialize. A clean kitchen enables disease-free food
production. Both are socio-technical systems that combine
soap, water, often machines and someone's labour. While
the exploitation of those involved in the production of soap,
water and machines is well recognized, we should also be
able to include exploitation of the other socially produced
resources: the water, the materials used for the soap, the
energy to run the machines and so on.

In many ways, the question of the exploitation of reliance
systems goes back to earlier transactional understandings
of exploitation, understandings that focused on the basic
terms of a deal. This is the aspect of exploitation we seek to

highlight – the abuse of the unavoidable requirement that our agency and freedom must be collectively produced and is not self-provisioned.

One illustration of this form of exploitation is found in the history of housing and African Americans in the twentieth-century American metropolis. During the immediate pre- and post-Second World War era, African Americans were largely confined legally and through violent social practice to a small number of generally inner-city or industrial suburban locations. This confinement was a result of government policy at virtually every level, the practices of formal professions such as real estate brokers and corporate entities such as developers, and was ingrained culturally in most white communities. The reliance systems view of exploitation diagnoses this as a form of exploitation in which the *purpose* of the production of the capacity of African Americans to house themselves was the production of *white* agential capacities. That is, the purpose of the system that produces substandard housing for black people was the production of white freedoms.[5]

This only broke apart when new cross-sector forms of exploitation were introduced. Urban renewal razed many of these communities, once wealthier and more powerful state and non-state actors saw that they could increase their capacities to make money by producing capacities for non-black people to live and work in those spaces instead of reproducing African Americans' capacities to house themselves in the existing substandard housing. Obviously, this is not equivalent to removing African Americans from exploitative housing relationships. First, some of these communities remained, but were simply worse off, riven by freeways and cut off from other parts of the city, and these core systems of exploitation persisted.[6] But in many other cases, African Americans were forced to use subprime or predatory credit in order to buy homes. Thus, a *new* reliance system – a financial system – was produced whose purpose was enrichment of the wealthy even as it was a necessary component of African Americans' capacities to buy a home.[7] Exploitation of reliance systems in the case of African Americans has always been multi-scalar and multi-sector, and has never stopped, even if the specific forms of that exploitation have changed over time.

Marginalization, or the exclusion from reliance
Young's notion of oppression as marginalization is a notion of *structural exclusion* from 'useful participation in social life'.[8] Young initially characterizes this in terms of exclusion from the 'system of labor', but she develops this to encompass exclusion from activities that are socially recognized as useful or productive or valuable. Because someone is excluded from contributing productively, they must be attended to by society and so are placed at the mercy of a variety of objectionable demands coming from those in power.

Marginalization understood in terms of reliance systems is exclusion from the agential capacities associated with the production of reliance systems. This involves not just being excluded from, for example, work associated with building infrastructure or producing commodities. Rather, it involves exclusion from the forms of agency associated with the capacity to produce the spatial contract itself. Chief among these would be the capacities associated with education and political participation. Those who are marginalized with respect to these capacities are not merely at a legal disadvantage, as are those whose voting rights are stripped. They are disadvantaged in the sense that even if they were legally permitted to participate, they could not. They lack an actual capacity even if it is formally guaranteed.

For example, because of the ghettoization and segregation of African Americans, an African American household in 1950s America could very well have had a decent and steady income, despite the many obstacles in the way of achieving this. But they would have been far less likely to be able to access quality school systems, secure financial services or enjoy reliable transport services. As a result, the capacities to educate oneself, to earn investment income and to travel through one's city are dramatically limited.

Further examples can be found throughout the world of these forms of space-based marginalization, from informal settlements to excluded suburbs, from stigmatized housing projects to the subtlest of marginalities which come from a change in post code – a weaker school district, a more overcrowded clinic, a less reliable bus service, poorer quality air or more polluted water.[9] All of these are exclusions from reliance systems that constitute forms of agency critical to the production of the spatial contract.

Exclusion from reliance systems does not have to be fundamentally spatial in nature. As we have referenced previously, a growing problem around the world is how the global majority is being marginalized from housing systems based upon the almost exclusive construction of luxury apartments in major cities. In both the Global South and Global North, central cities are being reconstructed around housing towers whose purpose is not the capacity for domiciling oneself. The action that they enable is purely a financial one – the storing of capital by the global elite.[10] In this way, a finite and often scarce resource, land, is recruited for the sake of producing the capacity to maintain wealth. Other resources – labour and materials – are also recruited for this end. Millions of people are excluded from a reliance system to realize capacities for housing themselves.[11]

Marginalization through exclusion from reliance systems can also occur when disaster and everyday history collide. In Puerto Rico, Hurricane Maria in 2017 wiped out many foundational reliance systems, including electricity. Five months after the hurricane, an estimated 180,000 people remained without power.[12] But as with Hurricane Katrina in 2005 in New Orleans, the hurricane is only part of the story. Puerto Ricans were already marginalized, in the sense that they lacked access to reliance systems constituting political agency. Puerto Rico has long had a very shaky power grid, heavily dependent on imported fossil fuels. The poor quality of this grid and the use of portable generators as backups were imposed on Puerto Ricans because they lacked the political agency to shape their own infrastructure. A similar story can be told about Puerto Rico's roads and ports. Thus when Maria hit, it not only affected this core reliance system by damaging power stations and knocking down power lines, but its impact on ports and shipping routes meant that fuel could not make it there.[13] Thus generators – which were already critical on an island where one could not always *rely* on electricity – failed because they ran out of gas. Cars and trucks couldn't transport the sick and injured, couldn't deliver food or water. A concatenation of events based on a deeper history of marginalization and exclusion resulted in the loss of reliance, not just the hurricane. The sustained damage caused by the hurricane was therefore just an exacerbation of the many exclusions that were consequences of a lack of political agency.

The conditions in Puerto Rico after Maria serve as an example of the *interaction* between exploitation and marginalization in the face of disaster, a phenomenon that Naomi Klein tracks in her book *The Shock Doctrine*.[14] Disaster has become profitable, as companies have learned to profit from the particular crisis that is a total loss of vital reliance systems. But the link between the two is much deeper, fused by the fact that disaster is now seen as a political opportunity to remake reliance systems in ways that exclude even more people, thereby diminishing people's core political capacities.

Right-wing ideologues saw Hurricane Katrina as a means of destroying a flawed if vital system of housing provision.[15] In Puerto Rico, ideologues and entrepreneurs see the ongoing crisis of reliance as an opportunity to change core systems in order to privatize them in the most dramatic way possible, not just selling off the grid but creating gated enclaves where the capacity to do anything with electricity is available only to the few.[16]

Powerlessness

Young's notion of powerlessness is rooted in the condition of working people who lack the sort of privilege, standing and autonomy common among those she calls 'professionals', or people in salaried jobs that typically require significant qualifications. This powerlessness includes but goes beyond what the philosopher Elizabeth Anderson details in her book *Private Government*, namely, the legal condition of one's life being dominated by one's employer. The further form of powerlessness is a social condition, in which one's voice over many small matters is limited.[17]

We affirm Young's analysis of powerlessness, but add to her focus on the *sense* of impotence and the concomitant *shame* a focus on the material bases of these emotions. In particular, on a reliance system analysis of powerlessness, what people lack are both the capacities to shape the conditions of their working lives and the capacities to make their voices effectively heard when resisting conditions either intentionally or structurally imposed on them. These capacities are realized, as all capacities are, in the reliance systems we collectively produce. The condition of the powerless, then, is the condition of those for whom these reliance systems are not available.

Once we focus on the material conditions driving the sense of powerlessness, we can begin to understand the lived experience of powerlessness more deeply. People's sense of their voice being either ignored or too weak to be heard reflects a failure of the collective production of reliance systems to realize people's capacities to express themselves publicly. The Brazilian educational philosopher Paulo Freire argued that this phenomenon, which we are following Young in labelling as powerlessness, often manifests itself in a kind of self-silencing, a kind of self-oppression.[18]

Trade unions and issue-oriented community groups can produce reliance systems that realize collective capacities for one's voice to be heard. This is an important supplement to the current near-obsession with online social networks as an amplifying voice. The capacities to organize and mobilize unions and other community groups may be extended by online social networks, but older organizational structures

– from meeting halls and paper agendas, to lists of members and their contact information, to notes on both members' and peripheral parties' enthusiasm and support, to means of transporting people from space to space, to systems that make demonstrations powerful (such as bullhorns and brass bands) – remain vital reliance systems through which collective voice is formed and expressed.

Other important reliance systems are those that realize capacities to access the clothes required to present oneself as a 'respectable' member of society or as a professional. This enables people to speak in a manner that is heard by others as, in some sense, authoritative, or to otherwise engage in the economy of respectability. Social standing, in short, is not merely the way people see someone, but is in fact a nested set of capacities associated with being able to make others see you as a person worthy of respect. A crucial element of this is the capacity to see one's own effectiveness as an agent, that is, the ability to *see* the exercise of one's own power. Whereas a corporate vice president can watch their employees organize themselves in accordance with his or her commands, and so can literally see the effectiveness of their own voice, the powerless have no such social mirror without reliance systems of the sort detailed in the previous paragraph.

Consider as a different example the case of protest. The capacity to effectively present oneself as a 'dignified protester' is more than a capacity to claim legal rights or to challenge the legal authority of the state. For example, in 1968 Memphis's African-American sanitation workers, who were as powerless as any worker in America, went on strike and, wearing their Sunday best, peacefully and bravely marched through angry white streets carrying signs with the message, 'I *am* a man.' The clothes and the signs, the material systems that their union and the Southern Christian Leadership Council provided, and so on, all did the work of claiming dignity. A law permitting protest is meaningless in the absence of these reliance systems.[19]

Powerlessness is often produced when the reliance systems

realizing these capacities are deconstructed or destroyed. This can occur under both 'normal' conditions and crisis conditions. For example, after Hurricane Maria hit Puerto Rico, the systems realizing the capacities of Puerto Ricans to participate politically were weakened. Efforts were made to undermine reliance systems that constituted people's capacity to express themselves.[20] This is different from marginalization in that it does not explicitly target people's capacities to engage in formal political processes. Rather, it targets people's abilities to be recognized as social equals.

But one must be careful. In an unhealthy spatial contract, the reliance systems through which marginalization and powerlessness are overcome can themselves produce marginalization and powerlessness. The long and tortured history of NIMBYism is but one example of this. In a healthy spatial contract, marginalization and powerlessness would not be produced anywhere, or at least it would not be produced unevenly. On the other hand, it is undesirable to have a direct voice with respect to every single reliance system. Ought people to be directly responsible for every aspect of food, water, transport, healthcare and so on? Would not most people prefer just to turn on the tap or the lights and have them work?

The response to marginalization and powerlessness is therefore not merely the production of ever more widely and evenly distributed capacities to shape directly every aspect of one's agency. Rather, there must be delegation that meets the conditions of the principle of transparency described in Chapter 1. Communities must collectively produce reliance systems that enable their members to learn about how their agential capacities are collectively provisioned in the first place. Educational reliance structures must be produced that generate and sustain capacities to engage effectively with members of one's various communities. But as we have noted, it is a mistake to demonize expertise, and it is a mistake to treat all technocratic administrative structures as objectionably anti-democratic. Where technocratic administrative structures weaken agential capacities and entrench uneven distributions of capacities, then there are reasons to object. Yet where technocratic administrative structures strengthen agency, for example, because they are effective, transparent and affirmatively responsive, they are key elements of a healthy spatial contract.

Those who do not suffer powerlessness also have trust in systems constituting others' power. They have faith in and understanding of the full system of collective provision, partially because this system enables *but does not require* engagement. Power in this sense is the ability to rely on collective provisioning without having to do it yourself. A political imagination that imagines direct individual or community power over all reliance systems is doomed to further fragment reliance systems; a renewed and healthier spatial contract imagines a politics of the future where one can rely on those engaged in the provision of specific systems to provision both effectively and without oppression.

Cultural imperialism
Young's fourth face of oppression is the first one she defines without labour at the centre. Developing the ideas of Lugones, Spelman and Fraser, Young defines cultural imperialism as 'the universalization of a dominant group's experience and culture, and its establishment as the norm'.[21] In an understanding that we follow, Young's view of cultural imperialism includes but goes far beyond questions of globalization and Hollywood, and is capable of capturing all the ways in which dominant culture is imposed tacitly or through force. Few cultures remain immune from struggles regarding the visibility, voice, recognition and power of non-dominant races, genders, ethnic groups, religions, sexual orientations or other challenges to normativity.

Cultural imperialism is realized in a lack of access to reliance systems that realize the capacity to produce popular and 'high' culture of one's own. This goes beyond a lack of access to the means of music, television and film production, to name a few obvious cases, and extends to the reliance systems constituting the education system. As has been well established, cultural imperialism can function as a tool of marginalization by provisioning only the dominant narratives and the dominant histories.[22]

Cultural imperialism of this sort directly undermines a healthy spatial contract by re/producing an uneven distribution of capacities for producing foundational reliance systems. The non-recognition of non-dominant groups in popular culture can impede the development of diverse expertise, let alone sufficient expertise in places where there are not enough trained professionals to operate systems. This ensures exclusion from control over the provisioning of many reliance systems. Furthermore, cultural imperialism directly undermines faith and trust in expertise, increasing powerlessness.

This is a finding consistent with much of the research on settlements in the Global South referenced in the previous chapter. Our fundamental understanding of how reliance systems are supposedly meant to work – what they are meant to do, who is meant to do them, how they should operate and be organized and governed and paid for – is often based on a very narrow set of cultural experiences in a very narrow part of the world. This is not to say that many of the ways of doing things invented in the North are not useful, and cannot be either adapted or even simply implemented in the South in effective ways. The culture is not the question, but rather the implicit or explicit imperialism, an often unthinking set of assumptions that many experts in both North and South are not trained to consider in a reflective manner.

Cultural imperialism can thus blind providers to various ways of intervening in their own systems. This is starting to change. Work in places such as the Indian Institute of Human Settlements, the African Center for Cities and places throughout the globe are trying to build new ways of cultural and technical exchange of ideas and expertise related to reliance, without having to deal with the imposed forms of knowledge production inherited from the nineteenth and twentieth centuries. Ideas for improving transportation systems, energy systems, street vending, public space and many other key systems are finally flowing from South to North, as actors in different sectors undo the limited geographies that colonial thinking imposed on so many of us.

Violence

Finally, there is the question of violence. Young emphasizes systemic violence, which is violence directed at members of a social group because of their membership in that social group.[23] In Young's view, violence can be direct and physical, or cultural, often intersecting with cultural imperialism.

The reliance system account of violence is different from Young's only in emphasis. Our focus is on the way that violence is deployed to exclude people from reliance systems. Violence is often systematically used as the primary tool for the destruction of human agency. The body is targeted with force, but the aim of the force is not to maim the body. Rather, it is to generate patterns of life that ensure that those marked with the threat of future violence lack access to or cannot provision for themselves any number of reliance systems.

An illuminating example of this is the growing problem of evictions, what Saskia Sassen refers to as expulsions and many other activists and scholars refer to as dispossession.[24] Even in cases in which people are rehoused, the more informal reliance systems that they depend upon for childcare, access to employment or cultural services, and many other formal and informal reliance systems are severed. As we mentioned in the previous chapter, rebuilding networks of reliance systems many kilometres away from the communities in which you built them can prove exceptionally difficult, whether you are being evicted from public housing in London, informal housing in Delhi or private housing in San Francisco.

A major contemporary vector of violence as a form of expulsion is privatization. As we have stated repeatedly, private is not inherently good or bad, and private providers are integral parts of many systems of provision. But what makes privatization as a process often so troubling is the violent way that it can sever people from the very reliance system that the actors involved generally claim to be improving.[25]

Eviction as violence therefore is not merely harm to the body. Rather, the point of this bodily harm is to remove people from one of the most foundational reliance systems, namely, the physical space in which to live. Wounds may heal, the body may no longer ache from the blows, but without a place to live, much less a place to call home, one cannot even perform some of the most basic actions – defecation, sleeping, having sex – without fear of shame, fines or imprisonment. In this way, slum clearance through baton-wielding policemen or legal eviction due to the privatization of public housing are similar forms of violence. They are both dismemberments of the material components of foundational elements of human agency. They destroy human freedom.

The struggle to constrain informal forms of violence typically involves the deployment of violence. Nevertheless, the regulation and suppression of violence is a vital reliance system. When it is working well, it lays the groundwork for expansions of freedom. Without a system that makes people feel safe, we cannot walk down the street, sit in a park, go to school or work, or even sleep soundly. Let us not pretend that safety is simply natural, any more than it is natural to have drinkable water or rapid transportation or healthcare. Safety is produced, and produced collectively.

But this system is not the same as the policing system, or the criminal justice system. For these two structures are only components of larger systems for the suppression of violence, alongside educational systems, social norms, family structures and so on. The challenge we face then is that this system is unique – it can and does produce violence, both as a means of suppressing it legitimately and as a form of criminality and violent oppression.

The other forms of oppression can be produced through violence but their mitigation can also limit violence. A settlement where people have power and voice, where they are not exploited and marginalized, where there is not cultural imperialism, is a settlement in which the reliance systems that control violence are limited in their ability to produce exploitation, powerlessness, voicelessness, cultural imperialism and marginalization.

Oppression and the spatial contract

Like the analysis produced in the previous two chapters, questions of exploitation and oppression in reliance can and should be used as part of any analysis of existing spatial contracts. Oppression is fundamentally ingrained in so many existing systems that we must consider it a fundamental component of our reliance systems. One of the many reasons why so many supposedly well-intentioned efforts at improving reliance systems fail is that they fail to consider oppression as

Table 4 Five faces of oppression in terms of reliance systems

Exploitation	The use by the powerful of the agency of the less powerful to reproduce the powerful's own agency, to the exclusion of the less powerful
Marginalization	The exclusion of groups from control over the provisioning of reliance systems
Powerlessness	The absence of reliance systems that constitute the capacity to have an effective voice in the community
Cultural imperialism	Exclusion from reliance systems that enable the production of one's own cultural forms
Violence	Dispossession from foundational reliance systems

fundamental to why reliance systems are unable to produce the types of freedoms that are needed.

Oppression is also clearly linked to the six principles of reliance delineated in Chapter 1, and not simply the principle of exploitation. The obligation to pursue the core purpose was made necessary by long histories of exploitation through a form of bait and switch – building housing to build wealth, not to build homes. Oppression as delineated above ultimately connects to all six principles – to issues of access, the strength of the system, transparency and planetary boundaries. If people are regularly oppressed in the five ways discussed here, how can they be asked or expected to contribute what limited agency they have to the growth and strengthening of collectively produced systems?

A healthy spatial contract thus demands that the agency realized in reliance systems be used to eliminate oppression, domination and exploitation in the production and provisioning of reliance. The common point around which we must rally is not the local or the state or the market or the commons, not an ideological imagination of how reliance systems are provided, not a scale or a type of place or a perceived lifestyle, not a dream of formal systems or a fetishization of informal ones. Rather, a healthier spatial contract depends on understanding systems and settlements as they are currently realized, and then reconstructing them in line with the six principles of reliance systems and with an eye towards overcoming the five faces of oppression.

Exploitative conditions weaken and often destroy the possibility of a healthier spatial contract. A fragmented, fractured politics of reliance only weakens the systems we all depend on for basic agency and freedom.

Notes

1 I. M. Young, *Justice and the Politics of Difference* (Princeton, NJ: Princeton University Press, 1990).

2 Ibid., p. 46.
3 Ibid.
4 N. Lichtenstein (ed.), *Wal-Mart: The Face of Twenty-first-century Capitalism* (New York: New Press, 2006).
5 For example, it produced the capacity of white slumlords to enrich themselves off a captive audience for housing.
6 M. Desmond, *Evicted: Poverty and Profit in the American City* (Portland, OR: Broadway Books, 2016).
7 Predatory finance is one of many forms of exploitative financial reliance systems, which include payday lending, cheque-cashing facilities and wire transfer companies that specifically target immigrants and those who live apart from people who depend on them financially. See M. Hudson (ed.), *Merchants of Misery: How Corporate America Profits from Poverty* (Monroe, ME: Common Courage Press, 1996); R. Rothstein, *The Color of Law: A Forgotten History of How our Government Segregated America* (New York: Liveright Publishing, 2017); A. R. Hirsch, *Making the Second Ghetto: Race and Housing in Chicago 1940–1960* (Chicago: University of Chicago Press, 2009).
8 Young, *Justice and the Politics of Difference*, p. 50.
9 The specific spatial forms, the particular reliance systems involved and the social group upon which the marginalization is based vary dramatically, but this connection between space, place and exclusion from reliance runs deep. This is yet another reason why we insist on seeing systems through the lens of human settlements, and vice versa.
10 They also prop up important construction economies that are key inputs into many different reliance systems. But these construction economies could be equally supported by the construction of houses that were actual homes, so the real output here in terms of reliance is the ability to store wealth.
11 As noted throughout, reliance systems can simultaneously realize different capacities. Sometimes the exercise of these capacities conflicts. These conflicts are often sites of oppression.
12 F. Robles, 'Contractors are leaving Puerto Rico, where many still lack power', *The New York Times*, 26 February 2018, https://www.nytimes.com/2018/02/26/us/puerto-rico-power-contractor.html (accessed 17 October 2019).
13 N. Klein, 'Puerto Ricans and ultrarich "Puertopians" are locked in a pitched struggle over how to remake the island', *The*

Intercept, 20 March 2018, https://theintercept.com/2018/03/20/puerto-rico-hurricane-maria-recovery/ (accessed 17 October 2019).

14 N. Klein, *The Shock Doctrine: The Rise of Disaster Capitalism* (Basingstoke: Palgrave Macmillan, 2007).

15 R. Brandes Gratz, 'Who killed public housing in New Orleans', *The Nation*, 22–29 June 2015, https://www.thenation.com/article/requiem-bricks/ (accessed 17 October 2019).

16 Channelling more electricity to harvesting bitcoin is the energy equivalent of empty luxury housing – the perversion of a core reliance system for another, less human purpose.

17 E. Anderson, *Private Government: How Employers Rule Our Lives (and Why We Don't Talk about It)* (Princeton, NJ: Princeton University Press, 2017). Young links this element of powerlessness to Sennett and Cobb's *The Hidden Injuries of Class*. See R. Sennett and J. Cobb, *The Hidden Injuries of Class* (New York: Vintage, 1972).

18 Taking together the reliance-systems-centred notions of marginalization and powerlessness, we can find it addressed by activism and writing about settlements under the aegis of French philosopher Henri Lefebvre's notion of the 'right to the city', briefly touched on in Chapter 1. The right to the city is not a specific right to something like housing or transport, but a right to be involved, to have voice, to have a say in the production of the place in which you live. Work on the 'right to the city' helps us migrate the concept of powerlessness away from a labour-centred definition like Young's into the realm of reliance and settlement systems.

19 In this way, overly legalistic conceptions of freedom are flawed. The capacity to be seen and to demand attention to one's dignity cannot be produced by legislation. It can only be collectively provisioned through the systems we have been detailing throughout this book.

20 See in particular the role of the Financial Oversight and Management Board, 'an unelected seven-member body that exerts ultimate control over Puerto Rico's economy'. Klein, 'Puerto Ricans and ultrarich "Puertopians"'.

21 Young, *Justice and the Politics of Difference*, p. 59. See M. C. Lugones and E. V. Spelman, 'Have we got a theory for you! Feminist theory, cultural imperialism and the demand

for "the woman's voice"', *Women's Studies International Forum* 6 (1983), pp. 573–81; N. Fraser, *Unruly Practices: Power, Discourse, and Gender in Contemporary Social Theory* (Minneapolis, MN: University of Minnesota Press, 1989).

22 The education system can also serve as a tool of marginalization and powerlessness by paying little attention to the specific learning cultures and needs of those doing the learning, impeding their educational progress. It can connect with systems of violence and interact with other reliance systems in what is discussed in the United States as the 'schools to prisons pipeline', whereby punitive and culturally tone-deaf educational systems are functionally fused with policing systems in problematic ways. See S. Gonsoulin, M. Zablocki and P. E. Leone, 'Safe schools, staff development, and the school-to-prison pipeline', *Teacher Education and Special Education* 35.4 (2012), pp. 309–19.

23 Young uses systematic and systemic interchangeably, but we will use only the term systemic, as it is clearer in referring to being 'off the system', as opposed to systematic, which has connotations of step-by-step consistency.

24 S. Sassen, *Expulsions: Brutality and Complexity in the Global Economy* (Cambridge, MA: Harvard University Press, 2014).

25 Klein, *The Shock Doctrine*. See Hodkinson's book in the Manchester Capitalism series about an infamous case of violence in this vein – the Grenfell disaster in London. S. Hodkinson, *Safe as Houses. Private Greed, Political Negligence and Housing Policy after Grenfell* (Manchester: Manchester University Press, 2019).

Conclusion: building a healthy spatial contract

Around the world, more and more people are realizing that we need to pay greater attention to the core systems we depend upon for survival. Not only are systems such as housing, transportation, food, energy, water, waste, education, healthcare and more central to our basic needs as humans, and to our basic freedoms, they are increasingly vulnerable to both exploitation by the powerful and disruption by the climate crisis. This book has worked to develop a three-part framework for thinking about the politics of these systems.

It is an intellectual framework which seeks to establish an understanding of reliance systems. Reliance systems such as water, transportation, food production, healthcare, housing and more enable us as humans to act, to have agency, and hence make us free. Freedom in this active sense of the term is realized in these systems, all of which are collectively produced. Even if we build our own houses, we do so with materials that we generally don't produce and knowledges that we did not create. The relationships between collectively produced reliance systems and human agency and freedom are what we call spatial contracts. A spatial contract is not inherently good or bad, or healthy or unhealthy, as we put it. The health of any spatial contract depends on the terms of the deal.

This book is also an initial analytical framework for understanding reliance systems. We develop three perspectives designed to examine reliance systems on their own terms, as they actually exist in the world, without falling prey to ideological approaches. The first is 'seeing like a system', an approach that uses systems thinking and various ideas from economics to see systems as dynamic and ever-changing, and as social and technical in nature. We highlight the need to understand them as vertical systems of provision and as ecological systems. Ideas from economics such as substitutability, rivalry and excludability can be redeployed if stripped of their ideological foundations. When one sees like a system, one recognizes that there is no inherently good sector, institutional form or scale. It depends on the system, place and moment in history.

The second part of the analytical framework is to 'see like a settlement', understanding how systems come together in space and place. Spatial contracts exist in all settlement types. We argue for an inclusive understanding of places – hence the language of settlement, which eschews terms such as city, urban, metropolis, urbanization, etc., which have multiple connotations of size, settlement type or culture. 'Seeing like a settlement' helps illuminate important divisions – urban/rural, city/suburb, legal/illegal, formal/informal – which can negatively impact the pursuit of a healthier spatial contract.

The third part of the analytical framework is designed to illuminate the varied forms of exploitation that can occur in reliance systems. By adapting Iris Marion Young's five faces of oppression to reliance systems, we can see how reliance on reliance systems is exploited, how people are excluded and marginalized from reliance, how they are rendered powerless in the provisioning of reliance, how reliance systems are often provisioned in culturally inappropriate ways, and how violence is a tool for dispossession and exclusion, increasingly intersecting with all the other forms of oppression.

Finally, this book is a political framework for reimagining the production and reproduction of reliance systems. We first argue that reliance systems need to become the centre of our politics. Healthier spatial contracts need to become a priority, and must be seen as 'high politics'. We must channel the current interest in all manners of infrastructure into a newly refocused politics that pays more attention to the systems that realize human freedoms.

We offer a set of six principles that can be used to determine the relative 'health' of a given spatial contract: the retention of the core purpose, the strengthening of the system, access and inclusion, elimination of exploitation, planetary boundaries and transparency. The political framework works in tandem with the analytical framework, as 'seeing like a system', 'seeing like a settlement' and the five faces of exploitation and oppression identify not only material but political barriers to a healthier spatial contract.

In the following section, we work to illustrate the framework in practice by examining two salient political conversations that directly revolve around reliance systems in some ways. These examples – universal basic income and the Green New Deal – involve different systems, different political lines, and vary in terms of their global reach. We purposely chose a more global example and a more regional (North Atlantic) example to highlight the scalability of this framework.

The spatial contract framework in practice: universal basic income

The idea of providing no-strings-attached money to all citizens or residents – a basic income, or universal basic income (UBI) – has gained significant political traction in various parts of the world in recent decades. Its proponents see it as a means to reduce poverty, as a more efficient system of distribution, or as a solution to the problems created by automation. Sceptics and opponents will point out numerous failings, from its role as a potential balm for capitalist exploitation to its impracticality or relation to the welfare state.

The philosophical motivations behind UBI are varied, but they mostly revolve around political commitments both to state neutrality between conceptions of what a good life would be, and to directly addressing certain structural forms of oppression. First, defenders of UBI insist that the state should neither value one kind of work over another nor value those who wish to work over those who do not wish to work. Second, defenders of UBI hold that an unconditional income goes a long way towards alleviating both discrimination against those who work part time and exploitation of those who work in poor conditions.[1]

Political theorists object to UBI on many grounds. The most relevant to us is that UBI is at best an intermediate measure and so is liable to leave the most vulnerable behind. As discussed in Chapter 1, Amartya Sen objected that an egalitarian distribution of, for example, wealth and income leaves vulnerable those who need more income to achieve a basic level of functioning. For example, someone who needs expensive prosthetics in order to walk may spend the entirety of their income disbursement merely to achieve a basic form of functioning. Meanwhile, everyone else is paying their utility bills and school fees for their children. What should be realized, Sen argues, is an equal distribution of basic capabilities, not basic income.[2]

A spatial contract perspective is a useful framework for a constructive engagement with UBI, pushing beyond ideological debates or divisions based on traditional political lines. The intellectual framework of the spatial contract forces us to recognize the limitations of money, whether in paper or digital form. Cash, which is certainly powerful, is not the all-powerful reliance system that some would believe. Cash can, in the right contexts, be a means of accessing reliance systems, but ultimately reliance systems must be *produced, not bought*. Cash alone does not realize agential capacities. This is the twenty-first-century version of the myth of King Midas. What cash buys are reliance systems and these are what make us free.

If cash is primarily a means to an end, the question becomes an analytical one. In any given system or settlement, to what extent does cash reliably facilitate access to reliance systems? For example, in India, some advocate for replacing direct food transfers with cash, which they claim will help lessen transaction costs and thus be more efficient, among other benefits. Sceptics raise the question as to whether the localities of the intended beneficiaries have sufficient access to the banking required by such a system. Are there bricks-and-mortar banks in their localities? Do they have reliable telecommunications systems so as to access mobile banking? As one cannot eat cash, the degree to which cash is an effective form for accessing the reliance system of food is a fundamental question.[3]

A more recent 'alternative' to UBI is the conception of universal basic services (UBS). This perspective argues that we should provide certain 'services' – what we would reframe as reliance systems – free of charge at the point of access.[4] Thus rather than providing cash to access energy, in South Africa all households with a grid connection are provided with 50kWh per month of electricity free of charge.[5] Similar proposals exist for housing, telecommunications and more.

As with UBI, the question of whether UBS is a good idea, or whether one is preferable to the other, should be a practical one, not an ideological one. A spatial contract perspective insists that UBS is not an alternative to UBI, simply an alternative mechanism for intervening in reliance systems, and that they can be compatible. Depending on the geography, moment in history and particular system, provisioning the system directly may be better than provisioning it through an intermediary such as cash. The South African example may work for those currently connected to the grid, but what about those not connected to the grid? How does it satisfy spatial contract principles of strengthening the system or increasing access?

The UBI and UBS questions also need to be analysed on exploitation grounds. While the liquidity and flexibility of cash can be a major asset, it can also expose people to serious predation and exploitation. Cash can be a positive or negative when it comes to all five faces of oppression. It can further exploitation, further marginalization, further power-lessness, be culturally inappropriate or ultimately be part of a system of violent expropriation – or it can have the opposite effect. Direct provision of reliance systems can similarly be a tool of oppression. For instance, in the Indian cash vs food debate, neither means is immune from oppression. Any proposed UBI/UBS system needs to take seriously this analytical framework, so that the relationship between UBI/UBS and questions of oppression is understood contextually.

From a political perspective, the spatial contract framework insists that conversations about UBI and UBS keep their eyes on the prize – healthier spatial contracts for reliance systems, which must become the central political goal. The six principles we offer each have a role to play in understanding the degree to which any UBI or UBS programme creates a healthier or unhealthier spatial contract. For instance, free energy can be a means of provisioning a healthier spatial contract for energy, depending in part on the degree to which it does or does not respect the principle of planetary boundaries.

The spatial contract framework in practice: the Green New Deal

The 'Green New Deal' is shorthand for a large-scale, Keynesian-style intervention whereby national governments would address unemployment, economic inequality and climate change simultaneously through a major public investment in retrofitting energy and related systems. The naming of this political project harks back to a set of policies enacted in the United States by the Roosevelt administration during the Great Depression, policies which became a key part of the post-war social contract we referenced in the Introduction.

The addition of the term 'green' indicates a new approach to this sort of massive Keynesian mobilization. Alive to the fact that reconstituting the original New Deal would further entrench a fossil-fuel-dependent economy and exacerbate climate breakdown, proponents of a Green New Deal in both the UK and the US have organized this new suite of national programmes around the aim of mitigating the threat of climate change. As the original New Deal was blind to the grinding racist and sexist oppression of the era, some Green New Deal proponents aim to avoid these mistakes through an emphasis on inclusion and voice.

The central proposals of a Green New Deal include large-scale energy efficiency retrofits of domestic and small commercial buildings, reforming energy systems to accelerate renewable energy deployment, ambitious targets on 'green jobs', large-scale reforesting of public and private land for both recreation and carbon dioxide sequestration, and retrofitting cities for low-carbon transport. There is also a strong theme of active fiscal policy and wealth redistribution within Green New Deal rhetoric. Funding for this programme is variously described as a mix of stimulus spending from money creation by central banks, state-underwritten low-interest loans, and substantially increased taxation on accumulated wealth.

From a spatial contract perspective, the fact that the Green New Deal is part of the contemporary moment is positive. It has focused our politics on energy provision, housing retrofit, transport and mobility – all critical reliance systems. At the same time, the debate around the Green New Deal is often mired in the politics of funding and jobs. Is it right or wrong to tax wealth at a given rate? Is it right or wrong to use Keynesian stimulus? How many and what type of jobs would it create? These conversations are important, and they need to be had, but they often leave little room for equally significant issues.

A spatial contract perspective adds three critical elements. First, it brings our attention back to the daily human freedoms that a Green New Deal would affect. For example, a Green New Deal would probably mean a change to the way in which we heat or cool our homes. It would aim to improve thermal comfort levels without burning fossil fuels. This means a change to heating and/or cooling practices in the home. How we achieve thermal comfort in homes is a big part of daily life. It structures our activities and practices more than we often appreciate. A debate over millions of jobs or billions of federal investment can obscure the fact that this transformation in heating and cooling systems would mean that most people in most homes would have to change features of their daily lives. Altering a heat source means planning to heat the home differently at different times, changes to how well clothes dry indoors, and changes to the physical appearance of properties. Recent work in the UK has shown how thoroughly individual households need to be engaged to consent to both the inconvenience of a deep household retrofit, and a change to the heating reliance system.[6]

The spatial contract around the capacity to produce thermal comfort, and the specific reliance system it yields, produces multiple freedoms: to dwell indoors, to work, play, cook, wash bodies and so on. The consent needed for a Green New Deal is not only the national politics of taxation, funding and job creation, it is also the consent to alter the reliance systems realizing these domestic freedoms. This demands its own politics.

The second element that a spatial contract perspective adds to the Green New Deal draws on our analytical framework. To 'see like a system' means understanding how the current system of provision will be affected by such an ambitious programme. How will the regime of heat provision in different places be impacted? What transitions are needed? Who wins and who loses? Which heating systems are 'right' when the reliance system can differ from neighbourhood to neighbourhood, even street by street? How a national Green New Deal comes to ground will be hugely complex.

A spatial contract perspective helps to manage and bound this complexity using the questions developed at the end of Chapter 2. The ecological, economic, scale and socio-technical elements of existing reliance systems can be comprehended.

Implementing the Green New Deal would mean a deep disruption to the existing spatial contract of domestic heat in both Halifax, Nova Scotia and Halifax, West Yorkshire, and using this framework we can explore how the same Green New Deal would differently affect the spatial contract in both places.

'Seeing like a settlement' also allows us to see the ways in which a Green New Deal would need retrofitting into an existing politics of landscape amenity, urban and regional politics over network access, and tensions over extending formal services to informal settlements. Using a spatial contract frame to see these issues, and building a political practice around this, would force us to contend with these issues explicitly. It will require a process of negotiation to build on this politics, as opposed to riding roughshod over it and damaging support for the programme.

Both 'seeing like a system' and 'seeing like a settlement' help us to build an understanding of reliance systems that can much more clearly explore the 'faces' of exploitation and oppression that a Green New Deal could ameliorate, create or exacerbate. Proponents of the Green New Deal in the US aim to avoid the racial impacts of the Roosevelt New Deal. In the UK, fuel poverty is an animating concern. Both conversations are pursuing a 'just transition' to a low-carbon economy, and having an explicit framework that brings our attention to this using our amended version of Iris Marion Young's five faces of oppression is a powerful starting point.

Thirdly and finally, the Green New Deal conversation has already placed reliance systems back at the heart of our politics, although not as explicitly as we would advocate. The political framework also forces us to ask whether delivering a Green New Deal will actually create a set of more healthy spatial contracts. One issue is the 'retention of core purpose'. How does a Green New Deal that is legitimized and supported on the basis of green jobs contend with the loss of employment in high-carbon sectors? Is a Green New Deal that creates more jobs better than a Green New Deal that is green[er] but with fewer jobs? Is this conflict in danger of overshadowing the core purpose of the reliance systems it disrupts? Is a heating transition that creates more installation and maintenance jobs better than a heating transition that is within the capacity of most homeowners to maintain?

A second question is 'strengthening of the system'. While current heating practices may be high-carbon they are largely very robust. Hardware stores stock replacement parts, expertise exists to maintain systems, fuel supply chains are resilient. Introducing new technologies and practices will cause an inevitable weakening of the system, *for a time*, and using the six principles of a healthy spatial contract allows us to see which political trade-offs are likely and explicitly address them as part of spatial contract politics.

Limitations and future directions for thinking

We recognize that there are many limitations to the spatial contract framework we have just presented. Some of these limitations are natural to any framework. We offer only two very brief illustrations above of the framework in use, not the full-length analysis that each would require. We also do not offer a detailed analysis of a given spatial contract in a given place – the energy system in North Yorkshire, food systems in India, transport systems in Mexico City, the policing system in a particular neighbourhood, etc. We hope to develop or see developed these and other forms of more detailed case study analysis in the near future.

There are also important limitations to the framework itself. These are areas in which we have not sufficiently addressed weaknesses and absences in our thinking, not addressed major debates that our work brings up, or not properly incorporated the ideas of others that could be useful in finishing the structure we have started to build. We fully acknowledge that the framework is incomplete, and that the list of limitations below is only partial.

Are certain human freedoms more important than others?
There will be instances when the re/production of one human freedom interferes with the re/production of another. How is this resolved? We have neither answered this question nor suggested a process for answering it. And yet any adequate account of a spatial contract must reckon with how to deal with these sorts of conflicts. This might take the form of a ranked list of agential capacities. It could also take the form of a decision procedure either for ranking freedoms, or for the ad hoc resolution of conflicts.

This territory has been well trodden by philosophers, political theorists, economists and others. For example, Martha Nussbaum has argued for a privileged set of central human capabilities. Others, such as Amartya Sen, explicitly reject such universalism about value. Sen, for example, leaves it to each political community to determine its own ranking of capabilities.

Intersecting and conflicting systems
Throughout this book we have used examples that treat reliance systems in isolation. Yet the spatial contract for transport clearly intersects with the spatial contract for housing. Where this is the case it is important to recognize that our starting point is not the system in question but the freedoms, the agential capacities that are realized in that system.

If the freedom to attend a place of work was once realized in the transport system but can now be realized in a telecoms system for home workers, then the system has changed but the human freedom has not. This only shifts the perspective of the analysis. It is now the telecoms network and compatible workspace in the dwelling that provision the agential capacity to attend work. This affects the transport system in nominally reduced congestion. It effects the energy system in thousands of home workers now heating a dwelling throughout the day.

Familiar problems in systems thinking are determining where to draw the boundary, and at what level of interaction between complex systems it is defensible to cease analysis. It is impossible to take a position on this outside of context. Instead we can only draw attention to these problems of 'system boundaries' and remain alert to the ways in which systems interact and unintended consequences abound.

Conflict between principles

There will also be conflicts between the principles of a healthy spatial contract. In some cases, strengthening reliance systems will only be possible by means that transgress planetary boundaries. Sometimes, ensuring that a reliance system retains its core purpose can block the expansion of access and inclusion to that system. How are we to manage such conflicts? Are certain principles important enough to dominate others, so that trade-offs are impermissible? Or could there be a weighting procedure that allows us to determine acceptable trade-offs between principles?

Like questions regarding the relative importance of different freedoms, theorists have long struggled with how to deal with tensions between principles. There are many routes to follow, from reducing conflicting demands to a crude utilitarianism of principles, to constructing intricate systems of ethics that serve as roadmaps for navigating these conflicts.

Property rights

We have intentionally left the field of property rights unexamined. The particular arrangements over exclusion, enclosure, benefits and damages are clearly central to understanding any spatial contract. We recognize that any political organizing around a spatial contract will have to question whether the current property rights governing a reliance system need changing. This invites a technical discussion about which basket of property rights is likely to work better for a given reliance system in a given place and time.

We have not explored the rich literature on property rights because it is often aimed at developing a rule set that hypothesizes which property rights work best for a given type of system – extraction from a fishery, use of common land, security in a gated community. But here our project is to advocate for an approach that starts by understanding the specific fishery, the specific common land, the specific gated community. Much as we worked to adapt ideas from economics, much work can and should be done to adapt ideas on property rights to the frameworks of the spatial contract.

Planetary boundaries

While we have made planetary boundaries one of our six principles for defining a healthy spatial contract, we have not defined these planetary boundaries. Typically these include climate change, ocean acidification, ozone depletion, freshwater use, the phosphorous cycle and biodiversity loss, but there are others. The term was popularized by Rockström et al. and its attendant literature demonstrates how aggregated human action, predominantly in the production and reproduction of reliance systems, undermines foundational ecological stability.[7]

Understanding how each planetary boundary is affected by each reliance system is important. Even with a short grounding in what each boundary is, we can start to see where and how different spatial contracts are going beyond ecological capacities. These boundaries are different for different places. Seeing like a system and seeing like a settlement can never completely deal with planetary boundaries. Developing an analytical framework for planetary boundaries needs not only to connect energy and material analysis to individual reliance systems, it needs to grapple with the moral dimensions of reducing consumption in some places while increasing it in others.

Reconciliation and restorative justice

A healthier spatial contract will require detailed understanding and acknowledgement of the role of exploitation in the provision of reliance systems. Our repurposing of Young's five faces of oppression is a step towards a practical analytical tool which can diagnose exploitation and oppression in any spatial contract. But this is insufficient for the purpose of overcoming the vast history of exploitation and oppression in most systems and most places. In many situations, it isn't even enough, as principle 4 requires, to reform existing practices to limit current exploitation, as past experiences have entrenched inequality of access, which violates principle 3. This is especially challenging given that long histories of exploitation may have limited or destroyed any potential faith that a better politics of provisioning reliance systems is possible.

What is needed is a model of conciliation or reconciliation for spatial contracts with exploitative dimensions, a means of building new faith in the possibilities of a healthier spatial contract. One way of doing this would be by further developing practices of restorative justice and reconciliation developed in post-conflict zones and criminal justice settings, but applying them to the production of reliance systems.[8]

Power
Attention to exploitation also raises the question of power and power relations in spatial contracts. So does the principle of core purpose, which was fashioned specifically to address the constant challenge in many spatial contracts of institutions using their power to push reliance systems away from their core purpose. While we briefly mentioned the work of scholars such as Deborah Cowen who have tackled issues of power and reliance systems head on, far more work could be done to incorporate these insights into a robust analytical framework for understanding power and power relations in spatial contracts.

Experimentation and innovation
Virtually every reliance system involves dynamic socio-technical systems. Experimentation and innovation are part of what makes a system dynamic, but experimentation can both disrupt existing reliance systems and even destroy them.

For example, in the Green New Deal example used above, a certain amount of disruption is inevitable. A more complete analytical framework would incorporate insights from scholarship that is alive to the distinctive threats that such disruption and destruction pose.

Expertise

Managing the production of reliance systems often requires technical expertise. Appeals to this fact have been deployed to justify both exclusion and marginalization. A healthy spatial contract, as we argue in Chapter 4, must both ameliorate such histories and aim to eliminate them going forward. We insist that people need to be able to understand the terms of a spatial contract. It is thus vital to produce reliance systems of media and education to maximize the collective capacities to access and understand these terms.

Yet there remain very difficult questions with regard to issues of expertise, understanding and participation in the production of reliance systems. How precisely is expertise related to the significance of one's voice in the production of a spatial contract? Are there ways to ensure *both* inclusion of the marginalized *and* that precedence be given to the voices of experts, at least in the governance of highly complex systems?

Process and organization

We have said very little about the types of social processes and civic organizing that are necessary to allow engagement and less harmful decision making in governing reliance systems, or processes of working through or modifying spatial contracts. This would require patient analysis of the individual contracts, and the people within them participating in a given spatial contract.[9] It would also require questioning what a spatial contract is to different communities, how the capacities produced by reliance systems are valued, and what changing them can mean.[10] Methods and means of organizing have often been undermined and marginalized by a ruling class bent on crude notions of utility, and new modes of organizing around spatial contracts are necessary. Following thinkers such as Monica Guillen-Royo, Elizabeth Shove and Frank Trentmann, we expect changes to even the largest national systems to require close engagement with individuals and groups to explore how individual reliance systems provision many basic needs, how they shape and are shaped by daily practices.[11] This work must be done in tandem with broader, systems-scale appraisal of aggregate outcomes. In short, process and organization around the spatial contract must be both bold in its ambition to retrofit for healthy reliance systems, and sensitive to the ways in which daily life can be deeply affected by even small changes to our urban infrastructurers.

Spatial contracts everywhere

We have worked hard in this book to present a non-universalistic framework for a twenty-first-century politics, one that does not depend on a particular imagination of how people should live. The spatial contract as a set of ideas rests on the fact that we all depend on other people to produce systems that make us free, save for perhaps a few true hermits. As we have said previously, this is not meant as a polemical statement, or a normative one, but simply a fact.

The analytical frameworks we have sketched out can give us an understanding of how specific spatial contracts in specific places are operating. Spatial contracts are everywhere, and we must learn to understand them on their own terms, instead of through the lens of ideology or imagined history.

But none of this analysis is worth much if we refuse the basic politics of this book.

For this framework to be useful, we must push our politics to pay more attention to reliance systems of food and water and healthcare and education and housing, of energy and transportation and policing and more. While the differences in how we discuss and define reliance systems matters, we consider ourselves fundamentally in solidarity with other political thinkers who push us towards a new political vision centred on infrastructure, urban systems, foundational economics and daily life.

We cannot hope to change our immoral and unsustainable planet unless we move beyond the ideologies and political frames of the previous millennia. The focus of our argument and debate has to shift to the systems that matter to our basic freedoms.

Notes

1 P. Van Parijs, *Real Freedom for All* (Oxford: Oxford University Press, 1995), and A. Levine, *Rethinking Liberal Equality* (Ithaca, NY: Cornell University Press, 1998).

2 Other philosophers, such as Nancy Fraser and Elizabeth Anderson, as well as Iris Marion Young, who defend a form of relational egalitarianism, would object that UBI does nothing to respond to differences in political power between members of the polity. That everyone has a minimal amount of cash does not really give the most vulnerable a significant form of political voice. As a result, severe deficits in political recognition and varied forms of oppression remain unaddressed.

3 J. Dréze, 'Evidence, policy, and politics', Ideas for India, 3 August 2018, http://www.ideasforindia.in/topics/miscellany/evidence-policy-and-politics.html (accessed 17 October 2019).

4 In reality this perspective is also not entirely new, as, for instance, the Indian direct food provision referenced in the paragraph above is essentially a UBS-type project. The difference between a 'good' and a 'service' is in this case irrelevant.

5 G. Ruiters, 'Developing or managing the poor: the complexities and contradictions of free basic electricity in South Africa (2000–2006)', *Africa Development* 36.1 (2011), pp. 119–42. We do not imply that 50kWh is sufficient for an average household, but the point is that the basic provision argument is illustrated by this example.

6 *Smart Systems and Heat programme: Phase 2 Summary*

    of key insights and emerging capabilities, Energy Systems Catapult, Birmingham, https://es.catapult.org.uk/wp-content/uploads/2019/06/Smart-Systems-Heat-Phase-2-Summary-of-key-insights.pdf (accessed 12 November 2019).

7 Rockström et al. 'Planetary boundaries: exploring the safe operating space for humanity'.

8 Although the term 'restorative justice' is generally used for specific processes within criminal justice or between specific victims and offenders, while reconciliation or political reconciliation tends to be used more for societal conflicts such as that in South Africa, Revd Desmond Tutu famously referred to the work of the South African Truth and Reconciliation Commission as restorative justice. *Final Report*, vol. 1, ch. 1, para. 36, cited in L. Adzik and C. Murphy, 'Reconciliation', *The Stanford Encyclopedia of Philosophy* (summer 2015 edn), ed. E. N. Zalta https://plato.stanford.edu/archives/sum2015/entries/reconciliation/ (accessed 17 October 2019).

9 H. Cottam, *Radical Help: How We Can Remake the Relationships Between Us and Revolutionise the Welfare State* (London: Hachette UK, 2018).

10 M. Guillen-Royo, *Sustainability and Wellbeing: Human-scale Development in Practice* (Abingdon: Routledge, 2018).

11 E. Shove and F. Trentmann (eds), *Infrastructures in Practice: The Dynamics of Demand in Networked Societies* (Abingdon: Routledge, 2018).

Index

agency 1–7, 13, 15, 24–8, 46,
  50, 54, 64, 96–7, 115–17,
  129–31
  materiality 29
Anand, Nikhil 5
Anderson, Elizabeth 123
Angelo, Hillary 98
Appel, Hannah 5

Benhabib, Seyla 38
Berlin, Isaiah 23
Born, Brandon 78–9
Brenner, Neil 100–1

capabilities approach 25–30,
  138, 145
Ching, Barbara 102
Cowen, Deb 4–6, 148
Creed, Gerald 102
cultural imperialism 126–8

deliberative democracy 9,
  12–13, 38–40

ecological ecosystems limits 44,
  67–8
  see also planetary boundaries
ecological limits 55–6
economics 55–6, 68–75
  commons 73–7, 82, 131
  foundational economics 10

mainstream (neoclassical)
  economics 63, 68–75
  neo-Marxist economics 75
excludability 55, 70–3, 81, 91,
  136
experimentation 148–9
expertise 39, 45, 64, 78, 96,
  125–7, 144, 148–9
  see also experts
exploitation 4, 6, 14, 43–4, 46,
  74–6, 81, 114–20

Fennell, Lee Anne 74
freedom 23–5
  capabilities approach 25–8
  materiality 28–35

Graham, Stephen 107
Green New Deal 14, 140–4
Gupta, Akhil 5
Gutman, Pablo 104–5

Hobbes, Thomas 7, 23
human settlements see
  urbanization

ideology ix, 12–15, 36, 47,
  55–6, 61, 68, 72–82, 91–4,
  108–10, 114, 122, 131,
  136–9, 150–1
incumbency 55–6, 59–63

Indian Institute for Human
    Settlements 98–100, 105–6,
    127
infrastructure 3–5, 30, 59–60,
    64–9, 109, 122, 137
innovation 80, 98–9, 148–9

justice 28, 36

Klein, Naomi 122

localism 77–8

marginalization 120–2
Marvin, Simon 107
Meadows, Donella 59
municipal services *see* urban
    services

Nussbaum, Martha 26–30

Ostrom, Elinor 73–5

planetary boundaries 147
political agency 122
power 148
    powerlessness 122–6
principles of healthy spatial
    contract 40–7
property rights 12, 37, 74,
    146–7
public goods 68, 70–3
Purcell, Mark 78–9

Rawls, John 25–6
regime 61–2
reliance systems 2, 11–12, 28–35
    functional v. material
        component 32–4
restorative justice 147–8
right to the city 13, 37
Roy, Ananya 101, 108

Sassen, Saskia 128
scale 12–14, 37, 56, 68,
    73–81
Schmid, Christian 100–1
Sen, Amartya 25–30, 138
Simone, AbdouMaliq 109
social contract 7–11, 35–7
socio-technical systems 56–63
Soja, Edward 92
structural injustice 76–8, 116
substitutability 34, 55, 68–70,
    81, 91, 136
systems of provision 13, 55,
    63–9, 77–80, 129, 136
systems-centred thinking 55, 68,
    75–7

universal basic income 14,
    137–40
universal basic services
    139–40
urbanization
    city v. suburb 14, 93, 97–101,
        136
    and illegality 93, 105–10,
        136
    and informality 2, 98,
        105–10, 136
    urban services 94
    urban v. rural 14, 93–104

Vaseduvan, Alex 109
violence 4, 23, 28, 35, 76,
    128–30

Wachsmuth, David 98
Williams, Michael 101
Wirth, Louis 97
Woods, Michael 101, 104

Young, Iris Marion 14, 115–31,
    136

EU authorised representative for GPSR:
Easy Access System Europe, Mustamäe tee 50,
10621 Tallinn, Estonia
gpsr.requests@easproject.com